Flying Under the Radar

Al Isley

Flying Under the Radar

Copyright © 2012 Al Isley

All rights reserved.

ISBN-10: **1463610920**

ISBN-13: **978-1463610920**

Cover by Anthony Isley

Al Isley

DEDICATION

This book is dedicated to my loving wife who stood by me through all the trouble and hardships I put her through. She managed to work and survive while raising my teenage son. And did a heck of a job of it.

CONTENTS

1	Belize	11
2	First Flight	23
3	Back in the U.S.A.	31
4	Cocaine in the U.S.A.	37
5	Celebrities in Flight	53
6	Mexico Flight	59
7	C.I.A. Flight	63
8	Jamaica & the Islands	69
9	Stealing the Plane	81
10	Selling to a Drug Dealer	83
11	Run for Jim Allen	91
12	Newsflash!	95
13	DEA Set Up	103
14	The Indictment	113
15	The Trial	119
16	Guilty	125
17	Going to Prison	131
18	California	143
	About the Author	151

ACKNOWLEDGMENTS

I would like to acknowledge the help of my friend and
author Jean Bailey Robor
and
designer Melody McBride of FlashbacksbyRed.com.
Without their help I don't know if I would have
ever finished this book.

CHAPTER ONE

Belize

I woke up in a sweat, hot and wondering where I was. I thought it was a Viet Nam flashback. As I came fully awake, I saw, in the moon lit darkness, I was in a small grass hut with dirt floors on an old army-type folding cot. Then I remembered where I was and why I was here.

My name is Jake Thomas from Louisville, Ky. I had flown in to the country of Belize with a high-paying passenger who wanted me to fly back to the U.S. with a plane load of pot. We had met earlier in the day with some people from the Columbian Cartel and had walked approximately two miles back in the jungle for a meeting. The people my passenger was meeting with were wanted by the authorities; staying out of sight was imperative. They were having a meeting in a small village in the jungle. I was not involved. I was tired and lay down for a nap.

Even at ten p.m., the weather was hot and humid. I got up and walked outside. The hut I had been sleeping in was part of a small village. One of the locals directed me two huts down to the guys in the meeting. I came in and was offered a beer to which I took right away. The frothy liquid felt good against my parched throat. The meeting was coming to a close. As it was late, they decided to spend the night here. It's not safe to walk through the jungle at night.

I had been flying this same guy on different flights for the past year or so. I would just tell the wife I had a charter and would be gone for a couple of days. I would call when I could. We had two children, a boy and girl, both in school. I was 45 years old and this was not the life I had planned. I was a very good pilot and I really didn't need to be doing this trip.

The next morning I woke up with birds singing and sounds of people talking mostly in Spanish. I walked outside. There were three kids, barefoot, kicking a soccer ball, a woman cooking over an open fire. My passenger, Jim Allen, also from Louisville, Ky. was outside smoking a cigar. I had met him through his brother at the airport in Louisville. I knew he dealt in drugs and was impressed he asked me to do a couple of flights for him. He was talking to one of the people from the Cartel. They called me over and Jim said, "Let's all have some breakfast." Sounded good to me.

It was cooler now. We walked down a small path to an open hut and sat down and ate fried bananas. They were delicious. Monkeys played in the trees. There was a small stream close to the hut and the gurgling water was a pleasant sound to wake up to. After downing some really strong coffee, Jim suggested we head back to the small airport where the plane was parked. It was near the house we had been staying in. It was an old colonial-style house almost on the beach, with a small runway good for small aircraft. We had rooms rented there. It was much more comfortable than the hut. We started the two-mile walk back through the jungle. As the sun climbed higher in the sky, the day was starting to get hot. It didn't help that there was no breeze.

Jim had originally planned for me to fly some marijuana he intended to buy here back to the States. But after he had met these guys from the Cartel, he discovered they had some cocaine they wanted to move. The one contact, a guy named Danny, was the Columbian go-between to a high up Cartel member, Jose` Ortega. Danny had about 210 kilos of coke from the Cartel and Danny's pilot was not available to go get it in Colombia. He wanted me to go to Colombia and pick it up and bring it to Belize. Then I could take Jim and his pot to the States as planned. I knew that getting caught with pot was not nearly as bad as cocaine. Jim so far has stayed away from it. I had no desire to transport it either. I had thought it too risky. But the money was good.

When I was about eleven years old I had my first airplane ride. My dad's cousin, who was a pilot, came home from the second world war and gave lessons at the local airport. My dad gave him two pounds of chicken livers to take my brother and me for a ride. He loved chicken livers. Dad raised chickens for a living and farmed. He was a hard working man and everyone liked him. Mom taught school and retired from the North Carolina school system.

My first time in that airplane is a vivid memory, even these many years later. Flying was it! We flew in a big yellow Piper Cub. Two seats, one up front and one behind. I got to ride in the front. I loved every minute of it. This is how I got the flying bug. I was hooked!

This guy Danny was a big guy over six feet tall and 250 pounds. Not too friendly. He had the reputation as a guy you didn't want mad at you. I didn't like him and felt uneasy around him. Jim told me he threatened to throw a guy out of an airplane because he thought he was a snitch. He kept a 45 automatic stuck in his belt. He looked like the type of guy who would kill you and not think anything about it. He wanted to pay me $20,000 for the run. Then I could take Jim and his load into the States to Kentucky. I had done this a couple of times when charter business slacked off. Jim usually paid me $30,000 for the marijuana run. Sometimes when I dropped down and landed on a road, it was off loaded in less than five minutes. Although I transported it, I didn't use the stuff and didn't care who did. But this was different. I had never been to Columbia and landing in a jungle was something I was not comfortable doing. In all my other flights I had checked them out before and looked at the site before landing.

I told Danny I would think about it. He wanted a quick answer because he was committed to the Cartel and had to get it picked up so he could move it. I felt the pressure. I looked to Jim. He wanted me to please Danny as he was a good contact to the Cartel. Plus, Jim now saw a chance to make so much more money with cocaine. Inside, I squirmed, wishing I had not made this trip.

I wondered what my wife and family were doing. I worried about them when I was away like this. If something should happen to me, what would they do? How would they get by? I had some money but most of what I had made was spent on a couple of airplanes. The kids were teenagers. My wife worked retail for an upscale women's store. We did pretty good. But I knew my life insurance would not pay if I was killed in a small plane accident. These are things that weighed heavily on my mind.

That night I thought long and hard about my decision. Even in the colonial-style house with all its amenities, I could hardly sleep. As the sun peaked over the horizon, I got up and prepared to meet Danny. When I saw him, I could tell by the look on his face that it would not go well for me if I disappointed him. But I had already made my decision. I told him I would go. He arranged for someone to go with me to show me the way. I was anxious. I just wanted to get this trip over. At least I wasn't flying it to the U.S. I knew that in most of these third world countries you could buy your way out of most anything. The authorities in the U.S. were different.

Danny's friend showed up the next morning. We checked the plane over good and departed. This guy handed me a pistol. He had his own automatic weapon in case we had to go down or ran into trouble on the ground. Just the thought of either scenario made me even more uncomfortable.

We were headed to a location near Bogotá, Columbia. He had given me a heading for Nicaragua. We flew over Costa Rica and Panama. The guy knew all the landmarks and after about three hours we flew over an active volcano. The glow of the red hot lava was fascinating and, for a brief moment, my anxiousness eased. A short time later we spotted a small clearing in the jungle. Just some trees and bushes cut down to land on. He told me to stay low so we wouldn't be spotted landing. There were other drug gangs that would love the get their hands on the coke. My nervousness resumed. *Why had I chosen to take this risk? What was I thinking?* My anxiety about landing on this strip in the jungle must have been evident.

Danny's friend glanced over at me and assured me it would be fine. I took a deep breath and began our descent. It was a really short strip and very rough. You might say it was the worst landing I have ever made. There were some small bushes too close to the strip and the prop cut them up. Pieces of brush were flying everywhere. I breathed a sigh of relief as we rolled to the edge of the strip. Then I turned the plane around so it would be ready to takeoff.

Four or five Columbians ran around loading the plane. All were armed with automatic weapons. They dragged duffel bags full of coke up out of the bush. Just like Belize, it was very hot and humid. No breeze at all. Thick bushes and palm trees lined both sides of the strip. I had to go relieve myself and went through some of the brush off to one side. It was well hidden; just six feet off the strip you couldn't see anyone. The jungle was very thick.

When I came back the guy in charge, Pedro, laughed and said I should watch it in the brush. There are things in there that could bite and sting you. That was the least of my worries. By now I was wet with sweat and still nervous about getting out of here.

The fuel and 210 kilos of coke were loaded without incident. Still, I was worried. That was only half the battle. I still had to get out of here. They tied down the duffel bags so the coke wouldn't move around in case we encountered rough air. Danny's friend was not going back with me. That was a relief. I didn't need his weight. I knew the engine in this heat would not produce full power. I didn't want to crash and never be heard from again.

Before I got into the plane, one of the Columbians came running. Sweat-soaked and breathless, he said another drug gang was headed this way and I should take off at once. We must have been spotted during landing. They didn't want to lose the coke and urged me to take off now. Now! The Columbians disappeared into the jungle. Sweat dripped off my brow. I jumped in and started the engine.

I started the take off roll. It was sluggish to say the least. The plane was bouncing and struggling for speed. I wiped the sweat from my eyes and held my breath, watching the end of the strip getting closer. At the last moment I pulled back and barely made it over the trees at the end. God, that was close. Now I could breathe. If the other guy had been in the plane I was sure we would not have made it off. I turned north east and climbed up to cruising altitude. It was much cooler up there.

Now I was thinking, *Why, did I ever agree to do this?* What if something happened to the engine on the way and I had to put down in the jungle? I tried to think about something else. I still had the pistol. I had some water; I drank about a pint. I was on a sixty degree heading; I knew that would be good for now. I had picked up a beacon signal from Costa Rica and was headed for it and settled back to relax. Finally, I could breathe.

While flying over Costa Rica the directional gyro went out. Now I had no good instrument to get the correct heading except the magnetic compass bouncing around in a liquid which is not that accurate this close to the equator. I checked the charts to see what the earth's magnetic deviation was in this part of the world. Guessing to be about 12 degrees west, I just headed east and knew I would hit the Gulf of Mexico and could fly the coastline up to Belize. I had plenty of fuel and charts of the area. Then a thought occurred: *What if I had to put the plane the plane down somewhere on a beach?* My Spanish was limited and I didn't know how friendly the people would be.

Still, the engine was running good so I just tried to put my fears out of my mind.

Back in Kentucky Jim's brother, Andy, was checking out the field where I would be coming in with the marijuana. It was located about forty miles southwest of Louisville, Ky. It was not an airport but a field that had been used before by us once in a while. Andy had flown in a load of pot and almost got caught. They had to dump it out. Fortunately, it was at night so it wasn't spotted. He got lucky. This was where I came in. Jim approached me and I was having some financial difficulties so I agreed to do one flight for him. Just one. That was a year and four flights ago.

A couple of hours later I spotted the small runway where we were staying. I made a call in code on the radio and it was clear to come in. I landed with no problem. Danny and two others came out to unload the plane. I went in the take a shower and rest.

I slept for about an hour and got up and walked outside. Jim and Danny were doing some coke and laughing, having a good time. They offered me some. I knew that snorting pure cocaine was very dangerous. In its pure form it is very strong. Dealers in the U.S. generally cut it three or four times; that is usually the way people use it. *No way*, I said. I didn't even like to be around it.

They were pleased I got back safely. Danny asked me to stick around and do some more flights for him. Just to move the drugs from Columbia to Belize. He would pay more. He had talked to Pedro after I took off. Danny had said he thought I was a better pilot than the one he had been using. Pedro agreed; he didn't think Danny's pilot could have landed and gotten out of that strip. I was the first one to make it out. That's when I realized these guys were ready to write me off if I didn't make it. That's why the guy that flew down with me didn't want to go back. He didn't think I could get it out of there. As short as the airstrip was, I'd had my doubts myself. It wasn't a scene I wanted to recreate. So, when Danny asked me to make more flights, I declined. I could tell he was not happy with my answer. Jim had not known this was the first time anyone had successfully gotten off this strip; Danny had given him the impression they used it all the time. He apologized to me. I didn't trust this Danny one bit. I just wanted to get out of there and get back home. Jim said we would leave as soon as his marijuana arrived, probably that night.

The next morning Jim's pot had not arrived. Danny said his pilot was not coming and he had to get this cocaine sold and pay the Cartel. He was furious. Danny said he wanted me to fly it to the States. Jim would be the broker for him and move it there. I told him *no way*. I agreed to pick it up for him in Columbia and that was it. He had paid Jim my $20,000 for that trip and I wanted to get out of there. Jim thought differently; he now had a chance to make lots of money if he got the coke in and moved it. Danny looked me straight in the eye and said, *"You'll fly it or else."* There was no question this guy was very dangerous; I knew his words weren't just an empty threat. I was beginning to get angry myself. I didn't sign up for this shit. Jim realized I was not comfortable at all with what was going on.

I walked outside, into the heat of the noon sun. Jim followed me out. He said Danny was offering $150,000 to get it in and any legal costs if I was caught. He said he only paid his regular pilot $100,000. It would be hard to turn down that kind of cash. I began thinking if I went the same route I had planned maybe I could get in undetected. Besides, if I refused, Danny would blow me away, not think anything about it and get another pilot. Still, even though he was offering a good price, it could be better. I told Jim to tell him it would cost him

$200,000 and any legal fees and I would do it. I had him over a barrel and he knew it.

Danny came over and started yelling at me. He said he was being very generous and he was tired of my smart ass attitude. I was scared shitless but tried not to look it. I told him that was the deal and I would leave in the morning. He stomped off with Jim following. When Jim came back he said Danny agreed and Jim would pay me when I got it in.

A few years before this trip, I was contacted by a couple of C.I.A. agents recruiting pilots. They knew I flew a lot in and out of the U.S. and to other countries and the Caribbean. We met and I agreed to fly after I talked it over with my wife. She said she was fine with it plus the pay was good.

I flew commercial with them to Miami, Florida to their location on the south end of the Miami Airport. The company was Air America.

I only made two flights with them and they told me how to sneak into the U.S. without being detected by the radar. I just had to drop down to about one hundred feet, about fifty miles out and the radar couldn't pick me up. Coming in from the Gulf there were lots of oil rigs out there that were as high as one hundred feet. Ships on the east coast also prevented the radar from going below one hundred feet.

One of the flights with them was to Nicaragua. The strip was raided by the government Sandinistas; we were giving guns to the rebel Contras. We got shot at and barely got out with the plane and back to Miami. I made up my mind then to quit with them. I was sworn to secrecy to not talk about what I had seen or done. This was a quite a few years ago and I am not worried about it now. Had I been 30 years old and not married I probably would have stuck with it. The thrill and excitement I liked. But I knew I had a responsibility to my family.

I went back to my regular charter business. I flew a lot of patients for the V.A. hospital in Louisville, KY. And this kept me busy at times.

With each drug run, knew I needed to get away from this business. I was dealing with dangerous people. I had been lucky so far. Many nights I found myself lying awake thinking of how I got into the drug business and why; it was often hard to sleep.

Al Isley

CHAPTER TWO

First Flight

One hot Sunday afternoon in July 1945 my dad took my brother and I to a small dusty air strip in Burlington, NC. My dad's cousin, Ed Harris, had just gotten out of the army air force as a pilot. He was giving flying lessons. I had always loved airplanes. I was about 12 years old and Dad said he would get us a ride. Dad raised chickens for a living and Ed loved chicken livers. So Dad cut a deal with Ed to take my brother and me flying. The payment was two pounds of chicken livers.

The airplane was a big yellow Piper Cub. The ride was a memory I will always have. We flew over lakes and towns. The view was more than amazing. The experience of flying even better. Ed even let me have the controls for a while. I wasn't nervous just excited. I was sold on flying after that.

Growing up in the small North Carolina town of Siler City was like most any small southern town. We didn't travel much except to my grandfather's farm in Burlington and to Myrtle Beach, South Carolina. We loved the beach. My aunt on my dad's side of the family was a nurse there. She was an army nurse in the war and moved to Myrtle Beach after she left the army.

The high school had a small sports program with baseball, football and basketball. We played the other small schools in the area.

During the two summers of 1949 & 1950 about 5 of us guys worked for a local contractor on the Outer Banks of North Carolina. There was a ship on the beach that had been there since World War II. While it was being towed down the coast it had been caught in a storm and beached there. The contractor had a contract to cut the ship up for scrap. He was looking for cheap labor and we jumped at the chance to go and live at the beach for the summer. None of us except one older guy had ever used a cutting torch. This is what we were to use to cut the ship up in pieces. After the older experienced guy showed us how to use the torch, with a couple of days of practice, we were experts.

The ship was located on the island near the community of Rodanthe, NC. That's near the north end of the island, the tip of the Outer Banks, with an abundance of lush flora and fauna. At that time there were about 10 buildings there. Now there must be ten times that. The ship was a LST from World War II. It had two large doors on the bow that opened up to let trucks and tanks roll out on the beach. It was about two hundred feet long. It took us two summers to cut it all up, down to the sand where it had sat. Needless to say we had a great time there. We had two pickup trucks that we drove on the beach at low tide. The exhaust on them was rusted out from the salt water. You could hear us coming from a mile away. On weekends we caught the ferry back to Kitty Hawk on the mainland and hung around the Wright Brothers

Memorial trying to pick up girls. We were in demand on the island as a lot of the guys our age had gone into the service. With the company of an abundance of available girls, we had bonfires on the beach almost every night. So, in our eyes, we did have an exciting childhood.

My hometown of Siler City is located in the western part of Chatham County near the center of the state. It was mentioned a lot in the Andy Griffith show on TV. "Aunt Bea" a regular on the show visited there one day. She decided it was a good place to retire and moved there in 1972. She and my mother used to go to the local Methodist church. Although most everyone knows her by "Aunt Bea," her given name was Frances Bavier. On December 6, 1989, a local police officer, who checked by her house every day (whether she was in or out of town) came by. She didn't answer the door. He went in and discovered she had died in her sleep. She is buried in the cemetery on the north side of town. She had two cats the policeman also took care of when she wasn't home. When she died she left everything to him, including the cats. She had no family and a couple of months after she died he left town and nobody seems to know where he went. Maybe she left him enough to retire on himself and is living on an island in the Pacific somewhere.

Later while in high school the war in Korea was in the news a lot. I was in the age group to be drafted. So I and four friends enlisted in the *new* Air Force. This was January 3rd 1951. It was now called the U.S. Air Force and not the Army Air Force. I just wanted to be around airplanes. I was sent to Lackland Air Force base in San Antonio, Texas for basic training. With the outbreak of the Korean War enlistments were high. The Air Force was filled with men coming in and didn't know where to put them. We were put in tents at first and then put in a condemned barracks they re-opened. There were still more men coming in than they had room to put them. We didn't get any clothing issued for the first two weeks and had to wear what we brought with us. I wore out a new pair of wingtip shoes marching everywhere. The news commentator Walter Winchell said if you have a son at Lackland, pray for him; if you have a son in Korea, write to him. I was later transferred to Sheppard Air Force base in Wichita Falls, Texas for training as a flight engineer and crew chief. Then the Air Force discovered they had lost our records from basic training and we had to repeat basic training again. After going though the same training we'd had at Lackland, we started mechanic school. After about eight weeks of school and more training I got a two-week leave to go home. When I returned I would find out where I would be stationed.

My dad was in the U.S. Marines after the first World War and I almost joined the Marines. Mom was afraid that if I did I would be sent to Korea. I decided I would go into the Air Force, not so much to stay out of harm's way but because of my love of airplanes. Once my leave ended, I returned to the base and, guess where I had been stationed? Korea. Actually, I went to Japan first, but the division I was assigned had a detachment in Japan and Korea.

We shipped out of San Francisco on the troopship "U.S.S Mann." We hit a storm about the second day out and I saw more guys than you can imagine puking everywhere. A couple buddies and I, thankfully, didn't get seasick. It's a motion sickness and it was everywhere. We had a green navy crew and most of them were sick. We were topside during the storm and were hitting the largest waves I had ever seen. The ship's bow would go under one wave and the props would come out of the water and shake the ship. It was over two and under one. The waves would brake over the bow and it's a wonder we weren't washed overboard. Everyone below was sick. We didn't want to go down there. In a day or two the storm had passed and we docked in Yokohama Japan.

Japan was nice duty. We were sent to a base at Tatuskawa. Japan is a pretty country and I saw a lot of it on weekend passes. We rode trains everywhere. Their public transportation system was surprisingly impressive so soon after the War. I was there about eight months and then I was sent with the detachment in Seoul Korea. While in Japan I did a lot of sightseeing. Met a lot of Japanese girls that spoke good English and we went on weekend tours of parts of Japan. Beppu, Japan was really nice with natural hot springs running down from the mountains into the hotels. The hotels had sunken tubs in the bath area. Relaxing in the hot water running into the tub was fantastic. We would ride a train to the towns and take a tour bus for the tours. The trains were cheap transportation and fast. A few months later I was transferred to Korea.

I didn't tell mom for a few months after I was sent to Korea. Just didn't want to worry her. My brother picked up on the no postage on my letters and mentioned that I was probably in a combat zone, Korea. I told him we weren't near the fighting. I lied. We could hear artillery shells going off day and night. Then a few weeks later a combat reporter asked a couple of us to pose by the airplanes. He took pictures and sent them to our hometown paper. Well, the cat was out of the bag because I got this worried letter from mom. She wanted to know where I was and was I alright. She thought I was still in Japan. The compound was just outside of Seoul Korea near the Haunn River. It's a major river that runs through Korea.

In the winter it was so cold the guys in our tent would go down to the Haunn River and find it frozen over, about a foot thick each year. We would stand on the ice and shoot at cans and bottles on the bank. We wasted a lot of ammo but it was fun. My buddy Roger Crilley had shot his last round and I offered him some more 30cal ammo for his carbine. He said, "No let's go back." Well, that night he was cleaning his weapon and found that the last round he fired did not go out of the barrel and stuck about halfway in the barrel. If you know anything about firearms, you would know that had he fired another round the gun would have exploded in his face. He turned it in and said that was the last time he was going to shoot anything.

We were flying missions and sometimes we would pick up ground fire on many of the flights. We could come back with fifteen to twenty bullet holes in the plane. We sometimes dropped supplies and troops. We also dropped leaflets asking the North Korean troops to surrender. We would remove the rear cargo door where a large speaker was mounted; a South Korean female voice would urge them to surrender. At the same time we threw out leaflets calling for surrender. We were shot at a lot from the ground and we shot back with our 30cal carbine. But the people in charge didn't think that was a good idea, asking them to surrender and shooting at them at the same time. So they wouldn't let us take any weapons except our sidearm, just a pistol. We landed on strips where a bull dozer would have pushed some trees out of the way; we picked up wounded. I didn't tell my mom all that. We had some good pilots assigned to our group. Some were airline pilots that were in the reserve and were in for a few months; then they would go back to the airline. Most couldn't wait to go back to their old job of flying for the airline. They were losing money while flying in the Air Force.

We had a pilot assigned to us that had a famous father: Eddie Rickenbacker, fighter ace from World War I. He later became the CEO of Eastern Air Lines. This was Bill Rickenbacker. He was a nice guy and could fly anything. I once sold him a pistol. A 9mm automatic my dad had sent me. I didn't like the 45cal that was issued to us. It only held 7 rounds in the clip and the 9mm held 14. Pop said the sheriff back home took it off a prisoner. Nice gun. Rickenbacker liked it and when I rotated back to the states, I sold it to him.

I almost shot a South Korean major with it one day. We had picked up about fifteen to twenty South Korean troops. As their officer in charge, I instructed them, with the help of an interrupter, what to do if they felt sick, how to use the sick sacs. I warned them not to puke in the floor of the airplane. Just before landing I checked the area near the back door and there was puke. After landing I stood by the door and said no one was getting off the plane until it was cleaned up. Apparently the major was the puker. He tried to push his way by me and I resisted. He put his hand on his pistol as though to pull it out. I was faster as I had practiced my fast draw. He knew he was beat. We stared at each other for a moment, eye to eye, and he put his pistol back. By that time the pilots had come back and asked if there was a problem. I told them, *"No problem."* The Major then ordered a solder to clean up the mess.

The plane was met by a little South Korean kid that did odd jobs and spoke English pretty well. We used him as an interpreter. We flew other missions just off the coast of North Korea to Che-Ju-Do Island. The U.S. Marines had a weather station there. It was north of the 38th Parallel in the Sea of Japan.

We flew in thanksgiving dinner to the troops November 1952. While there the radio man and I went for a walk near the western edge that had some scrubby brush near the shore. I had to take a leak and walked down to some brush near the shore. Two men jumped out with a rifle; scared the shit out of me. One motioned for me to put my hands up. They hadn't seen the radio man; he was still walking up the hill and out of sight. They were dressed like the North Koreans I had seen. I saw a small boat in the water that they had probably come over in from the mainland. One of the guys walked toward the boat. The one with the rifle turned around and said something to the other guy. I drew my pistol and fired two times; he went down and the other one ran. Then I ran back up the hill. I wore a western type holster and had practiced my fast draw a lot. No one heard the shots and when I got back to the ops building I reported what had happened. They sent a squad of Marines to investigate. They came back and had not find anyone or the boat, only some blood on the ground and evidence of footprints in the sand. They apparently were spies sent over from the mainland. That's the last I heard of them.

CHAPTER THREE

Back in the U.S.A

I was shipped back to the States in 1954 and went to Hunter Air Force base in Savannah, Ga. for about two years. I re-enlisted for another four years in headquarters command, Bowling Air Force Base in Washington, D.C. Now that was good duty. There were more girls in Washington than I had ever seen. We used to go downtown about 5 pm and park and watch them getting off work. Most worked for the FBI or Navy department. If you found out where they hung out at night you could sell the information. I had more dates every week than I could have ever imagined. The downside was, there were so many I would forget their names when we were out. It was a little embarrassing. I was selling cars at a Lincoln Mercury & Edsel dealer part time. Remember the Edsel? I had a Lincoln demo and was it a girl getter. Every time I came in the base front gate the MP's saluted me, assuming I was a high-ranking officer because enlisted men couldn't afford a car like that. My dad loved that car. After about a year I took his Mercury in trade and gave him the Lincoln. He still had it when he died. My mother said it was too big for her to drive and she traded it for a smaller car.

Another buddy there in Washington was Jim Sullivan. Jim and I both got our pilot's license. Both of us owned a small plane. It just happened we both got the same type of airplane: single engine with twin tail and two passenger side-by-side seating. It was called an Ercoupe, nice little plane, and we could fly all over Washington DC with no problem. We used to fly right over the White House and the Capitol; now try it and you will get shot down. My mother came up for a visit and I flew her down the Potomac River so low we were level with Mt Vernon, George Washington's home, and people on the ground were waving to us.

Jim was hoping to get a position with an airline and we lost track of each other after I was discharged. I guess he probably did get on with someone. I had been best man at his wedding and it was kind of funny because he was Catholic and I had never been in a Catholic church. I was raised in Siler City, NC a Methodist. There were no Catholic churches near there. The Priest did everything by the book and no slacking on kneeling on one knee when he started the service. He commented that I did it better than the Catholics that were there. I was just learning and he jumped all over the others and told them to watch me. We all had a good laugh over it.

The Ercoupe airplane I eventually sold to a radio and TV personality Arthur Godfrey. He had a farm in Leesburg, Virginia and one of my air force buddies and I used to fly in there a lot. Godfrey saw the plane there one day. He made me an offer I couldn't refuse. I sold it. He was a pilot and had flown a lot of different planes. But he loved mine and wanted it to commute back and forth from Washington to his farm in Leesburg.

One of my barrack buddies went on to fame later in life. Jimmy Dean. Yep, he is mostly now known for his sausage. Jimmy had a band and played Saturday nights at the Oxon Hill, Maryland firehouse.

We had a great time there. He later got on a local TV station and then to the Ed Sullivan show; soon he was making movies, hit records and sausages.

I met a very nice girl at the dances and we dated for a few months, almost got married. Just couldn't pull the trigger and do it. She wanted to and I guess I wasn't ready to settle down. Her dad owned a Chris Craft boat dealership on the Potomac River up in Washington. We went boat riding every weekend. I was worried I couldn't support us on my pay. That was the only excuse I could think of. I was discharged a short time later and promised to write but didn't.

We flew generals and Pentagon people around and after four years I got out and worked at a variety of jobs. While still in the Air Force in Washington I got my private pilot's license and enjoyed flying by myself in the Ercoupe. The Air Force had a flying club and had 4 airplanes in Maryland near Washington DC. Now that I had sold my airplane I joined the flying club to have something to fly. Once I had to make an emergency landing. The reason I had to find a place to land, quickly, was that the engine had been heating up. I landed in a soybean field in Rich Square, N.C. It was 1955. The plane had almost stopped when the wheel pants over the wheels filled up with dirt; it locked the wheels causing the plane to go up nose down. It hesitated for a moment and finally flipped over completely upside down. I didn't get hurt but the airplane was messed up a bit. I crawled out the door and a farmer in the next field ran over to help me and to see if I was hurt. I was just a little shook up. He gave me a ride to town. I called the base and a buddy came down the next day and picked me up. Now I had a problem. The club's airplane was upside down in a bean field. I called the club president and he called the insurance company. They sent a truck to pick up the plane and bring it back to the airport for repair. I got out of that with no cost to me. Thank goodness.

Some of the generals I flew with found out I had a pilot's license. They quit taking a copilot and I did most of the flying; they logged all their time as first pilot. They didn't have to split it with another Air Force pilot. One of the generals tried to get me to go to cadets and become an Air Force pilot. I almost did. The Vietnam War was breaking out pretty strong then and I thought if did it would be a good chance I would wind up flying in Vietnam. I elected not to go.

After my four years in Washington I was discharged and went back to North Carolina. I almost stayed in. I had second thoughts about when I got out that maybe I was making a mistake. Instead I returned to North Carolina and worked as a car salesman in Greensboro. I did that for a while and then took a job in St Louis, Mo. with a freight forwarding company at the St Louis airport. Still around airplanes again but just wasn't making the money I wanted. I found a job with an insurance company as a claims adjuster. While working for the insurance company I met a girl that worked in the office. We dated for about a year, got married and had two wonderful children. I'm glad I waited.

During this time I also worked part time for a Private Investigator doing insurance claims on insurance fraud cases. The company had a VW bus that we used for surveillance work. Sometimes we sat in it all day waiting for the claimant to show. We would take pictures if they acted like they had no injury. I had to testify in court a few times on some of the cases. Still, I wasn't going anywhere with my life and began looking for something else to do. I interviewed for another job with a company that transported checks to clearing centers such as the Federal Reserve Bank, calling on banks to set up the service. The service for the banks allowed them to get their checks cleared faster and cut the float down. I was transferred to Chicago, Illinois and after two years there I was asked if I would like a transfer. I was ready to get out of Chicago and was sent to Louisville, Kentucky in 1970.

While in Louisville I obtained my commercial pilot's license and instrument rating. I started flying charter and selling airplanes part time. I managed to save enough to buy a plane. A Cessna 210, a real nice single engine airplane. It had four seats and it was fast. As a family we flew almost everywhere we went, including visiting my folks in North Carolina and my wife's family in Illinois. During vacations we flew everywhere we went, even to Mexico and the Caribbean. My kids were great flyers. I had been promoted to branch manager but flying was my life. So I resigned from the company and decided to make flying a business.

I started flying a lot of people out of the states on vacation and everywhere. Bahamas, Mexico, you just name where you wanted to go and I would fly you there. I was going places I always wanted to see and getting paid for it. I would figure the rate I wanted to charge and go. I sometimes leased a twin for the over water flights. I was one of very few pilots in the area that would fly out of the United States. I had to fill out paperwork for other countries and to turn in to customs when I landed. I had all the necessary papers and forms needed to clear in and out of customs for various countries like the Bahamas, Jamaica, Mexico, Cayman, Belize and others. I had the flight hours and experience so I was in demand. I finally traded my Cessna for a twin engine piper Aztec. This was a reliable twin engine airplane and had a good pay load. But it had only one door to get in and out of the plane. I really liked this plane but it was limited in carrying passengers and not any freight.

I had a contract with a local ambulance company and flew a lot of veterans for the Louisville Veterans Hospital. So I traded the Aztec for a Piper Seneca that has a large loading door in the rear of the plane. Now I had a nice twin engine airplane that allowed me to remove all the seats except the pilot & copilot's so it would hold two stretchers side by side in the rear with me and a paramedic in front to tend the patients. Most of the patient flights were only one stretcher and a relative if one wanted to go along.

Somehow, from my first flight in a small airplane to my time in the military to transporting people I found myself in a situation as dangerous as my time in the combat zone in Korea.

CHAPTER FOUR

Cocaine to the U.S.A

The drugs were hidden in the dense jungle near the airstrip. They had taken them out of the house. Danny was there and said it would only take ten minutes to load. The plane was already fueled and ready to go. I would be leaving on Sunday like I had already planned. Only I would be carrying a different cargo. I planned to take the same route anyway. Jim wasn't going back with me; he was flying back commercial.

So Sunday morning we went out to the plane and they proceeded to load it. I checked the load and pulled a net over it to secure it from moving around in rough air. I planned to leave about ten o'clock and that would put me approaching the U.S. ADIZ zone about two o'clock. The ADIZ (Air Defense Identification Zone) is an area that stretches about 50 miles from land out to sea. When your plane entered that area you would call and identify yourself because you were on military radar. They would give you a code to put in your transponder that would indentify you till you get into the U.S. border.

The plane was ready to go. I had checked it over twice with the checklist. We ate breakfast. I got a jug of water, two bananas and took off at ten o'clock. I took off, going out over the water, barely clipping the tops of a palm tree with my landing gear before it retracted all the way. I knew I was close but it wasn't until later I found out how close.

The weather was good here but thunderstorms were forecast for the gulf coast. I smiled. This is what I wanted. Radar picks up the rain and if you can come in around the storms they can't pick the airplane up on the radar.

I was flying at nine thousand five hundred feet. My over water life raft was right behind me and I wore a life jacket in case I had to ditch. The time was looking good after I left the Mexican coastline. Speed check was good and, if the wind held, I would be approaching the ADIZ at around 2 pm as planned. After about an hour I ate a banana and drank some water. The air was smooth and clear; I had the autopilot on and it was doing a great job of flying the airplane. *I should have brought a book to read.*

It's really boring flying over water unless you have someone to talk to. You sometimes hear a noise or a vibration that really isn't there but your imagination plays tricks on you. You have no landmarks to look at, just water. Sometimes you may spot a ship but you don't want to get too close to it. They might just report a sighting of a small airplane. Without many distractions, you daydream a lot.

On this day, the water was smooth and beautiful. About an hour later I saw a small boat like an inflatable such as I had in my emergency pack right behind the pilot's seat. I dropped down to a lower altitude and saw no one in it. It could have come off a private boat that was towing it. I was climbing back up to 9500 ft. and noticed the charts in the copilot's seat appeared to be moving. *Was I still daydreaming?* I picked up one and, *"Holy Shit!"* It was a snake, sticking his head up and staring straight at me with his little black beady eyes. The rest of his body lay on the floor; he was still and not coiled to strike. Now I'm at

9000 feet in a small plane over the Gulf of Mexico and I can't just jump out and run. I knew most jungle snakes were poisonous. He must have crawled into one of the bags while they were laying in the jungle. I figured as we reached a higher, cooler altitude it had crawled out, looking to get warmer. It continued to stare at me. I was desperately trying to figure how to get rid of it without getting bit. The autopilot was flying the plane so that left me free but free to do what? I had no idea. It looked to be maybe three feet long. I slowly reached behind the seat and got a small bath towel I kept there to wipe the windshield off. Slowly I brought it up and put it in my left hand. I threw it over the snake, grabbing it just behind the head. I quickly opened the door on the copilot's side with my other hand just enough to toss the snake out, towel and all. I was surprised the snake didn't coil around my arm; maybe it was cold or just high on cocaine. I was so scared I didn't know if I'd been bit. If the snake had bitten me and it was poisonous I would be dead before I could get help. I checked my hand. It looked ok. Now to get the door shut. It was almost impossible due to the air pressure inside the cabin. I finally got it shut but not latched; it was noisy with the air. I just had to live with it. I was hoping there was not another snake hidden back there that might come out and roam around. Then, for some reason, a snake joke popped into my head. *"A guy was sitting on the bank of a river, fishing, and needed bait. A snake swam by with a frog in his mouth. The guy, knowing it couldn't bite him with the frog in his mouth, grabbed the snake behind the head to get the frog for bait. He got the frog but wasn't sure how to release the snake without getting bit. He had a bottle of Jack Daniels Whisky and pored it down the snake's mouth. The snake rolled its eyes back and went limp, slipping back into the water.. A short while later the guy felt a nudge on his foot. It was the snake with two frogs in its mouth."* Too bad I hadn't had a frog or Jack Daniels to pacify the snake!

I had planned to fly into the states just southeast of New Orleans. Lots of oil rigs out there. There were hundreds of them. Helicopters were constantly flying back and forth between the oil rigs and the U.S. shore line. I could have really used a GPS like they have now but they didn't exist then. Then I would have known exactly how far I was from shore and the oil rigs. On that day I saw cloud buildup ahead and, as I expected, thunderstorms. Not solid but scattered along the coast, most of them toward New Orleans. I could fly in between them and feel safe knowing I would not be seen on radar. Today you can't do this. Satellite tracking along with radar would pick up the plane as it left South America, and track it all the way to the U.S.

I thought I was getting close enough to spot some oil rigs. Sure enough I spotted one about five miles away at my ten o'clock position. I knew there would be more soon. I started my descent to about one hundred feet. Now more rigs were popping up on the horizon. These rigs reach out close to a hundred miles from the U.S. shore line. After I passed a few I started to circle around two or three but not close to any of them. I flew a north east heading until I could pick up a VOR beacon. This is a navigation beacon on a certain frequency. When I cross-referenced two of them, I got my position. I was about fifty miles out. I slowed my speed down to about ninety miles an hour. I then dropped down to fifty feet and got altimeter settings from New Orleans center and the height of the oil rigs, about one hundred feet high. With the snake still on my mind, I wondered if changing altitude and temperature would produce another visitor. I kept my feet off the floor. Just in case.

I saw a couple of helicopters flying around from the rigs. This was good. A few minutes later I could see the coastline. I got my position and I was just southeast of Grand Island, Louisiana. I turned to a heading straight into Bay St. Louis or Gulfport, Mississippi. I didn't see any more aircraft in the area and I made a landing approach to a small airport and touched down then back up and continued northbound. If the plane had been picked up on radar they would assume it had landed and another one had taken off from the small airport. I then climbed to five thousand feet and leveled off and switched the fuel tanks to the main tanks. This would be enough to get me to Kentucky. I kept a lookout for anyone following me. There were still a few storms; I flew around and in between them. About a half hour later I did a circle just to check my six to see if I had a tail. It looked ok and I continued on to Louisville.

Three hours later I was just southeast of Louisville and picked up the Bardstown, Kentucky Beacon. I flew straight in on it and made a radio call on a pre-assigned frequency. I got an answer right away. No conversation just code words, meaning everything was ok. The small grass strip was really just a field near Mt Washington, Ky. Weather here was good. I had left the thunderstorms back in northern Alabama.

About five miles out I made a full circle looking for a tail and saw nothing. I then started my decent to about twelve hundred feet. I flew directly over the field and saw a pickup truck near the entrances to the field. No other cars were near the field; everything looked clear. I landed and shut the engine down. A guy I had seen with Jim came running out and the truck pulled up. Another guy got out. I didn't know him. They started to unload the coke. It was all in two kilo bricks, packed in three duffel bags. It took them less than five minutes to put it in the back of the truck and covered it with a tarp. They jumped in the truck and left as I was cranking the engine up. I took off and headed for Bowman field in Louisville. I taxied down to the T-hangers and put the plane inside the one Jim had rented. As I checked the plane I discovered a palm tree limb stuck in the wheel well. The palm tree I clipped with the gear on takeoff from Belize. I pulled it out and took it with me to dispose of later. I did not want a palm limb from Belize connected to the plane. I shut up the hanger walked to my car and went home. I was really tired and hungry.

It was almost dark when I landed; it was dark when I got home. The wife was glad to see me. She didn't know where I had been and thought I had a charter to Florida and to the Keys. My daughter was on a date but my son and I talked for a while before I took a shower and went to bed.

The next morning after breakfast the phone rang. It was Jim, wanting to meet for coffee. We met at a local restaurant; he was happy. He said to follow him over to his house so he could pay me. I, on the other hand, wanted to get paid before he or his people that off-loaded the coke got busted. I took one heck of a chance and this was to be my last run. We discussed over coffee that he was thinking about another run in a week or two. Many pilots have made a lot of money doing this but I was not going to get greedy. I just didn't want to chance it again. I had enough now with the Columbian run to Belize and on to Kentucky. I really didn't want to get more involved. I could still do my charter work to keep busy. I could see that Jim was getting greedy and dealing with cocaine to make more money. I think the local DEA knew he was dealing in marijuana but he wasn't high enough on the list of really serious drugs; they were letting him slide for now. But, when it comes to cocaine, they will find out who is doing it locally and go after them. Or if they bust someone with the drug, they might roll over and testify against Jim in court that they got it from him. Then there are the two guys that off-loaded the coke; they could finger me and then I would be brought up on charges. Still, I didn't think they even looked at me during the unloading. I stayed in the airplane ready to start the engine when they finished, and I wore sunglasses and a ball cap.

We got to his house and went inside. I met his wife before we went down to the basement. Underneath the house were PVC pipes that were for water and sewer. Most any house looked the same. Well, some of his pipes were fake, didn't go anywhere. He took the cap off one large pipe and reached up in there and started pulling out bundles of cash. All ten thousand in each stack banded together. I don't know how much was in there. He counted out the two hundred thousand for me; I was amazed. He put it in a paper sack and handed it to me. I now had the twenty thousand dollars from the Columbia to Belize run and I didn't want to take any more chances. I told Jim I really wasn't interested in doing another run. I had been lucky so far, getting in without being caught. Pilots who get in a few times without being caught get greedy; they keep trying and that's when they get caught. Law of averages, keep it up and you will get caught. Jim was hoping I would do another one. He trusted me and I appreciated that. But now he had to get another pilot he could trust. One that was capable of getting a load in without getting caught. He said he could get the drugs from Columbia to Belize ok. Danny had a pilot to get them that far. Getting to the States was the problem. He also said Danny had two people he wanted to get to the States. They would pay $35,000 to get them both in. No drugs, just the two people. I didn't want to do it because they were probably Columbia Cartel; after landing in the U.S. they could shoot you and walk away without it costing them anything. I told Jim I might know someone; I would let him know in a day or two.

Loading wounded in Korea on the aircraft, evacuating to hospitals in Japan, circa 1952.

Outer Banks, NC - LST (Landing Ship Transport) ship was beached in a storm after WWII near Rodanthe. I helped cut it up for scrap. Circa 1949

Bill Rickenbacker, on right, with Col. Althaus. My tent is the "Lazy Eight" in the background. Seoul, Korea airbase. Circa 1952

My first airplane, 1957 Ercoupe. Sold to radio personality, Arthur Godfrey.

I had just come back from a mission in Korea. This is the compound where we lived in Seoul, circa 1952.

College Park, MD – Airport outside of Washington DC, circa 1958, where I rented a plane.

Thanksgiving Day, 1952 - After the altercation with the North Korean that I shot.

Al Isley

CHAPTER FIVE

Celebrities in Flight

In 1975 to 1978 I was doing a lot of charter flying for different companies in Louisville. I flew all over the Midwest and South. Each time I either leased a twin engine piper Aztec or flew the company plane.

Some of my passengers were running for governor. One of them made it, John Y. Brown, who then owned Kentucky Fried Chicken. One of the trips with Mr. Brown was to Hazard, Kentucky. And it was a hazard just to get in there. It was a small airport in the eastern Kentucky mountains a large coal mining area. When we flew in there was a massive amount of ground fog. We could see the tops of the mountains sticking up through the fog. I knew we were on top of the airport but I told Mr. Brown we couldn't land due to the fog. I suggested we go to Lexington, rent a car and drive to Hazard. He agreed. "I would rather be the John Y. Brown that was late than the late John Y. Brown."

Also, I flew for a U.S. Senator who shall remain nameless. As of this writing, he is still in Washington. I flew a lot of movie and TV actors that came in to appear in a theater in New Albany, Indiana. One was actor Doug McClure. He got his start in *The Virginian*, a TV series. He was playing in the Derby Dinner Playhouse in New Albany, Indiana. His fiancé, Diane, was with him. She was from England and needed to renew her visa. When she entered the U.S. she only asked for 90 days. She should have asked for 6 months. It had expired and she was about to be deported back to England. The Immigration Department was not nice about it and they had to do something quick. I suggested we fly to Canada, re-enter the U.S. and get another visa. He agreed and the next morning we left for Windsor, Ontario. My wife went along to make it a foursome. We landed and waited for their customs to come out. When the agent came out Diane started said the only reason we had come to Canada was to have her visa renewed. Suspicious, the customs agent told us to wait. He went back inside and checked with his boss. Now knowing her visa had expired, they denied her entrance to Canada. He said she would have to go back to England. We were back to square one. So we loaded back up and headed for Detroit just back across the river. Doug warned Diane to not open her mouth when customs came out. The U.S customs could do the same thing and deny her entrance back into the U.S. Two guys came out in a van and asked, "Who's the pilot?" I said I was and they gave me a card to fill out. They assumed we were all U.S. citizens and then one of them recognized Doug. They asked him for his autograph and gave us a ride back to the terminal. Still, we had not solved Diane's problem.

A few days before, she had talked to an immigration official in Indianapolis, Indiana. She said he and been helpful and urged her to call if she needed help. She did and he told her to contact the airport immigration head there. He filled out some paperwork and had one of his agents take it over to Windsor and mail it back so it would appear she came in from Canada. Plus he renewed her visa for six months. Mission accomplished. We got back to Louisville late that night. We all went to dinner then home for some rest. We spent time with them for a couple more days until they left town for California. We exchanged Christmas cards for a couple years and then I lost track of them. I found out Doug died in 1995 of lung cancer.

Mickey Rooney was another celebrity I flew around for a week or so. He was a great guy. We got to know each other well and Mickey invited me to play with him in a celebrity golf tourney in Indianapolis, Indiana. Foster Brooks was sponsoring it. We had a great time. He is a fun guy to be around. When he was to leave Louisville for Akron, Ohio, he couldn't get a direct flight. The only flight he could get was to Cleveland where he would rent a car and drive to Akron. He was playing *Capt. Andy* in the stage version of *Showboat*. I was leaving the next day for an airport in Pennsylvania to take an airplane up and pick up another plane to come back. I asked if he would like me to drop him off in Akron. He almost hugged me. He said for my wife and I to come up after the show started; he would leave tickets for us. After the show we could come back stage and then all go out to dinner. We did. His agent, Jack Craig, joined us for dinner at a very nice Polynesian restaurant. That was the last time I saw Mickey. I have since seen him on TV commercials.

Another star was Tom Poston; he was a regular on the *Mork & Mindy* show on TV. He played the drunk that lived upstairs. I was taking him to Cincinnati, Ohio to promote the dinner playhouse in New Albany, Indiana. I took a lot of the stars that appeared on stage in the dinner playhouse to Cincinnati when they were booked for a 15-20 minute appearance on a morning breakfast show. Then I would fly them back to Louisville. It was about a 20-minute flight. On this flight it was raining with low ceilings. I was making an ILS instrument approach to Cincinnati airport, really concentrating on the approach when Poston picked up the mic and said, "What's Sparky Anderson doing now days?" Anderson then was the manager of the Cincinnati Reds Baseball team. The Cincinnati tower didn't answer and Poston commented, "See, they never pay attention to you." He was a dry humor comedian. He later told me he was a fighter pilot in North Africa during the war.

He and his brother flew British Spitfire fighter planes; they were the only Americans flying British aircraft there.

Another celebrity was Grady Nutt. He was a local guy. Grady was a regular on the *Hee Haw* TV show. He was always in the barber shop scene; off screen he was an ordained Baptist minister. His church was the Broadway Baptist church in Louisville. On one of the flights with Grady we were headed for Franklin, Tennessee for a lunch speaking engagement at the local Junior Chamber of Commerce. We hit a terrible snow storm just south of Nashville. It was solid whiteout. I couldn't see anything and it looked solid all the way to the ground. Visibility was zero. I knew the Franklin airport did not have a precision instrument approach. That meant landing there was out of the question. Fortunately the snow wasn't sticking to the wings.

Grady realized how bad the weather was and I suggested we go back to Nashville, land there and he could rent a car and drive down. He agreed. I contacted Nashville approach and asked for an ILS (instrument landing system) into Nashville. I was cleared for the approach. It had to be one of the tightest approaches I had ever made. Visibility was zero and I flew the glide scope right down to just above the ground. I saw the strobes just before the runway lights and followed them in. As soon as I crossed the runway end lights I cut power and touched down. We were in about three inches of snow. I told the control tower we were down and they announced that the Nashville airport was now closed. They couldn't see us and told me to turn off at the next taxiway and follow the truck with the strobe light to parking. That approach used my entire instrument training at once. I was mentally beat. Grady rented a car and did make it down and back the same day; the storm cleared and we flew back to Louisville that evening.

On another trip I had leased one of the local flying service airplanes. It was a very nice Beech 58 Baron that I had flown before when we landed at Nashville in the snow storm. Grady elected to sit in the rear seat and relax on the way. I taxied out and was cleared for takeoff. I got about fifty feet in the air. There was no more runway. Suddenly the right engine had a very loud backfire. I lost power in that engine. I quickly identified the engine and pulled back the throttle on it, reducing my climb a little. There's an old pilot saying that if you fly enough you will have an engine quit on takeoff. Thank goodness this was a twin engine. The plane seemed to hold its own with about 700 ft a minute climb. I began to feel confident that I could turn the plane around, make it back to the runway and land. I punched the mic button and told the control tower I had an engine problem. They responded with "We heard it; take any runway you want." I found out later a magneto on the right engine had come apart inside the engine. I made a slow turn and the plane climbed nicely on the one engine. By the time I got settled on the downwind for landing, I turned and looked back at Grady. I told him we had to go back and land. Grady said, "Okay." He never moved the magazine from in front of his face; it was upside down. I guess he didn't want to see if we crashed. We laughed about it after we were safely on the ground. We finished the flight with another plane.

I flew Grady a lot on his speaking trips. We became great friends. One day he called the local flying service to schedule a trip. They knew I flew him and they paged me. I didn't answer it because I was going to western Kentucky to pick up my daughter from college for the weekend. Not being able to reach me, the flying service found two other pilots to do the trip. Grady was going to Alabama for a speaking engagement and return the same night. As I was getting into my plane to go get my daughter, the pilots walked by, said they had a trip and didn't know where yet. I knew both of them well. I left and didn't think anymore about it until the next morning when I walked into an aircraft repair hanger. The owner looked surprised, "My god, I just heard you got killed last night." I said, "What?" Grady Nutt's plane had gone down the night before. He was dead.

God, I was shocked. What a loss. Both pilots had been killed in the crash also. The weather had been bad as they entered Alabama. I knew one of them was not the safest pilot. I had checked him out on the plane they had used; he had forgotten a lot of items on the checklist. It seemed to be typical for him and I had gotten onto him about it the few times I flew with him. This time, he had not removed the control lock pin before takeoff; the plane pitched up. They couldn't get the nose down. It stalled and crashed. The plane was a B-55 Beech Baron and if that pin is not removed on the preflight control check and pressure is applied to the control wheel on take off, you cannot pull it out. This was in November of 1982. It's a real shame to lose a friend and a man of God like Grady. He was a very entertaining comedian. I still have four or five records of his performances. I just wish I had taken the call, made the flight and picked up my daughter the next day. Maybe if I had, Grady would be alive today.

CHAPTER SIX

Mexico Flight

I was contacted by a local Flight Service to call a certain individual that wanted someone pick up his plane in Mexico. After calling the man I realized I knew him somewhat from just hanging around the airport. He had a Piper Aztec that he had flown to Mexico and had a fuel pump go out and wanted me to go pick it up. As far as I knew he was a local businessman and not connected to drugs. He was willing to pay me one thousand dollars plus expenses to go to the Mexico City airport and fly his plane back. I agreed. It sounded like a good clean deal.

I was to fly down on a commercial airline to Mexico to pick up the plane. No hurry. So after flying to Miami, Florida I was connected to *TACA Airline a Guatemalan* airline. Now this was a new experience. The plane was an old Boeing 727 that should have been retired long ago. The carpet was dirty, smelled and I may have been the only American on board. It rattled and shook but soon we were off. They served some pretty good salsa and chips on the flight.

We arrived at the Mexico City airport which is on a mountain top. Elevation is approximately 8500 feet. The runway is about 15,000 feet long to accommodate large aircraft. I checked in customs and they knew about the plane I was to pick up. My customer had made good arrangements for me to spend the night there and leave when I was cleared.

Customs said the Mexican Airlines were on strike in the country and there were no flights to be had within Mexico. If I wanted to make some money they had people who would hire me to fly them within the country. They told me the Lt. Governor of the state of *Tabasco* was looking for a charter and that he paid well. "Sure, why not?" They called his office and I spoke to him; his English was a lot better than my Spanish. He wanted to leave the next morning to go to a sight-seeing inspection tour and planned to be gone three or four days. I quoted him a price and he agreed. We would meet in the morning at the Customs at the General Aviation terminal. That's where the plane was parked. I went out and inspected it and ran the engines. Everything looked fine. It had a six place seating and good radios.

We met the next morning. He was very polite and had his wife and another couple with them plus two small children about 7 to 9 years old. They all were going on the trip. With only six seats, I sat one child in his mom's lap and we departed for a small town in southern Mexico. He was very good at directions plus I had good charts of Mexico. Fortunately, the Mexican air traffic controllers spoke English fluently with hardly an accent.

After flying for about an hour the kids had devoured three boxes of fried chicken. There were chicken bones and paper all over the floor in the back. We arrived at a small airport near the Nicaraguan border. There was no control tower that I could see. As I approached to fly over to get a handle on the runway and any wind, there was none. So I made a standard approach, lining up with the runway. I was about $1/8^{th}$ of a mile out and saw another plane coming to land from the other direction. Quickly, I pulled up and turned left to give him room to land. His was a much larger plane. A twin engine with a 25-passenger capacity and it appeared one engine was not running. As he touched down he swerved to the right and the right wing looked as if it hit the ground. We saw two people get out and walked away. The right gear looked like it had collapsed. I could tell he was far enough down the runway that I would have no problem landing; his wing was sticking up so I rolled up under it. We parked and got out just as two taxis drove up. That's typical.

My passengers didn't seem too interested in the wrecked plane.

Everyone, including me, got into the taxies and the Lt. Governor told them where to go. We went to a local prison and were met by the warden and staff, all of whom were very nice and polite. He took us on a tour of the prison which ended at his office. It was very nice with a huge desk. While in there he offered me his phone to call my wife if I wished. I needed to call her and let her know what was going on. At times it was hard to call out of Mexico if the international operators were busy. But he had a direct line. So I took advantage of his offer and called her. She asked where I was and, since she asked, I told her the truth: "I'm in a Mexican prison." After a moment of silence, I heard a soft, "Whaaat?" When I told her it was a joke, she was not amused. But she was glad it was only a joke.

After about an hour we left to return to Mexico City. After making a call from his office, the Governor found he had to return.

When we landed, he paid me cash and said he enjoyed the trip. I did too. I spent the night at the Hilton, toured the town and left the next morning for Kentucky.

Al Isley

CHAPTER SEVEN

C.I.A. Flights

In 1976 I bought an Aztec of my own from an ad in a national trade paper, having sold the one I had. The owner was in Canada and was flying through Louisville, Ky. on his way to Tennessee. He stopped by and we made a deal. I discovered the aircraft was in nice shape. It had been well maintained. It had high time on the engines but they still ran well. I thought the plane would be worth a lot once the engines were overhauled. I flew it for a few months, also leasing it out and chartering. But I wanted another plane more suitable for passenger comfort. I needed one with a rear loading door like a piper Seneca. So I decided on a plan. I'd get the engines overhauled and sell or trade it for another Seneca. A plane with new engines is much more attractive to sell than one with high time engines.

I found a repair shop in Chino, California that had the best price on overhauls including the cost of taking the plane there and back. I took it out and left it there for about four weeks. The overhaul shop paid my airline ticket round trip to get home and come back to pick the plane up.

On my trip out to Chino when my position was just north of Albuquerque, New Mexico, I saw my first UFO. It was a little after midnight. My altitude was about 12,000 feet. It was a smooth flight and the sky was clear; there were lots of stars that you'd never see from the ground because of the haze. A beautiful night. I kept watching a light moving up and down about my ten o'clock position; then it would stop then move forward at a great speed, then stop, then move back and stop. I called Albuquerque center. I was on their radar and asked if they had any traffic in that area. They said they weren't painting anything out there. Just then a Delta airline commented and said they were looking at the same light and couldn't make it out. The light then took off going forward and up at high speed and soon it was out of sight. Just for the record, I was on oxygen and knew I wasn't seeing things in the night. The rest of my flight to California was uneventful. I landed in Chino and spent the night. I turned the plane over to the engine repair shop the next morning and they took me to the Los Angles airport for a flight home.

The shop called about three weeks later and said the plane was ready and checked out fine. On the return trip to pick up the plane I took my wife along and we stopped in Las Vegas for a couple of days before picking up the plane. I like Las Vegas. It's lot of fun whether you gamble or not. There are lots of shows and sights to see. My wife hit a slot machine jackpot for $100. When we were ready to go, I called the engine repair shop and one of the guys flew my plane over to pick us up; it was nice and a good checkout for the new engines.

They did a great job on the overhaul. They put new turbo chargers on both engines and they ran perfectly. The turbos had the power to get up to a high altitude faster. It also had a built in oxygen system. I really would liked to have kept this plane but it was not suitable for my needs. We had a nice flight back to Louisville Kentucky with a stopover at the Grand Canyon airport. We took a tour of the canyon before heading home.

About a week later a guy called saying he was from Florida. He wanted me to meet him in a local motel and discuss some flying trips. We agreed to meet the next day for lunch. Two men showed up. The one I had spoken with said he was based out of Miami International airport and worked for Air America. He said they were recruiting pilots. At that time *Air America* was a CIA airline. He knew I was experienced in flying the Caribbean; if I took the job some of my flying would be to various South American countries. They had airplanes in Miami that we could use. The pay was really good. I wouldn't ever have to worry about customs coming back to the U.S.. He asked me to fly commercial to Miami the next day.

I discussed it with my wife before calling him to confirm. He said he would meet me at the airport the next morning and we would go together. In the motel he had shown me his government ID proving he was a federal agent. So, what the heck; it sounded good. I talked it over with my wife again and she agreed that it seemed like a good opportunity. We flew to Miami the next day.

Their office and planes were on the very south end of the airport. It wasn't as nice as I expected. I met a couple of their pilots and they weren't as I expected. A grungy looking bunch, some older than me and some my age. At this time Oliver North was in the news a lot. After we talked logistics about the flights to South America everything was secret. We couldn't discuss any cargo or flights with anyone outside of their group. They had checked me out and I had a top secret clearance from the Air Force. After four days I got to see a couple of their planes; they were old cargo planes, no markings on them, just the small numbers painted on the tail. I was set up to fly with one of their pilots. I had met him the first day. After checking the manifest, before we left, the plane was loaded with boxes marked as farm equipment. So far everything looked legitimate but I still wondered about farm equipment going to Nicaragua.

The pilot's name was Ed. He was one I had met the day before. Ed looked to be in his 50s. I didn't know much about him except that he had been divorced. He was a pretty quiet guy.

We were off at 0700 the next morning in a C-47, DC-3 or *gooney bird* as some call them. The engines ran good and the plane appeared to be in good shape. I did the preflight as I was trained to do in the Air Force. I was very familiar with this type of plane. I had flown on them in Korea. Guess that is why I was selected to go on this flight. Ed didn't talk much. I still wondered what was really in those crates on board. We went around Cuba. I noticed he was not on the radio much. After about six hours we were over Nicaragua and still the name of Ollie North came to my mind.

Finally Ed was on the radio with someone and we approached a remote strip in the jungle about 4000 feet long. The old gooney bird could land and take off just as I had done in Korea. We landed and were met by about three old army 6x6 trucks. There were about 8 people whom I would guess were Nicaraguans. One American was speaking Spanish to them. Another operative for the company, I guessed. They started to unload the crates. Ed finally told me these were small arms and ammo for the Contras; they were against the Sandinista government in Nicaragua. The United States was backing them in their war.

Covert stuff. It was exciting but I really didn't know what I was getting involved in. Besides, I was married with two kids. Should I really be involved in this? The adventure was intriguing and exciting. I figured if I was single with no family I would have no problem sticking with it. Now that I was older, with family responsibilities, I had my doubts if this was something I want to do.

A tanker truck came up and Ed and I refueled the plane. The truck left and Ed and the other operative were talking in low hushed tones. Afterwards, he handed me a pistol and belt to put on. Some of the others had rifles. We took time to have sandwiches and coffee without much conversation. We were about ready to leave, just waiting for some cargo that wasn't there yet, when one of the Contras drove up in a jeep, yelling something in Spanish. Ed and the other guy yelled for us to get into the air ASAP. The government Sandinistas were near and must have seen us land. What I didn't see at the time was the Contras in the bushes; they were there for support. Ed and I jumped in the plane and started the engines, spinning around and heading toward the runway. There was no preflight check and balls to the wall for takeoff. As we were rolling I saw the Sandinista in two trucks, firing at us. That's when I noticed the guys on the ground firing back with automatic weapons. I closed the side window as we lifted off. Ed made a sharp turn to the left to stay low and away from the attack.

We didn't climb up until we were about 10 miles away from the strip. How they made out, I don't know.

We didn't talk much en route. We did talk a little about the arms we delivered and didn't bring anything back. We didn't have time.

Back in Miami we checked back into the motel. I guessed they kept rooms there all the time. I called the wife and let her know where I was telling her I would let her know when I would start back home. The next morning we checked back in at the hanger. Ed came over and asked why didn't I go back home. He said he would be in touch with me. Apparently the landing strip was now compromised and couldn't be used again. They would have to find another and wouldn't need me for a while. I was given another week's pay, in cash, and airline ticket home.

I got home late that afternoon. Of course the wife had questions and I made up a story about a local flight to Aruba and back to Miami. Inside, I was beginning to question my decision to stay involved. I decided I would have to decline any offers from Ed and go back to what I was doing. It was too risky for a man with a family. Ed didn't have anyone. He was divorced; maybe he just liked the thrill and adventure.

About ten days later he did call and said they had another landing strip. I told him of my decision not to continue. He said he understood. Of course we discussed the secrecy of everything we did. I didn't know much anyway. I guess that's how they wanted it until I was committed and had a few more missions under my belt. I still had my twin piper Aztec to fly. So that was my claim to fame as a CIA operative. No black ops. Or spy missions. Darn.

By now I had almost quit flying outside of the U.S.. I had heard I was getting a reputation of being a possible drug smuggler. Pilots who flew a lot out of the U.S. down past Florida were rumored to be in the business. I didn't need that reputation, so I had pretty much quit and only took flights in the U.S. At least for awhile.

CHAPTER EIGHT

Jamaica & the Islands

One of the local operators on bowman field in Louisville called me and asked if I wanted an out of the country charter. Three people were in Jamaica and couldn't come back on a commercial flight. They were from Nashville, Tennessee. They had purchased a lot of souvenirs and the airline wouldn't take them. They had called Nashville and no pilots were available that had flown out of the U.S. The Nashville base operator called the flight service in Louisville. They told him about me. I called the people in Jamaica and set up the trip after agreeing on a price. I didn't have a twin engine plane then so I leased one from a friend. It was an older Piper Aztec but had reliable engines and, when push comes to shove, that's what counts. It had long range fuel tanks on it so stopping for fuel wouldn't be a problem.

I left the next morning headed for Miami, Florida for a refuel stop. The weather looked good all the way. I arrived in Montego Bay, Jamaica late that day. I met my passengers at the hotel. There were three men from Nashville and they had a lot of Jamaican cultural items to take back. I had taken out the rear seat in the plane to make room for the items. It was a six seat plane and I didn't need the rear seat. I spent the night and we left the next day. I filed a flight plan with the Jamaican air traffic control. They were supposed to transmit the flight plan to the Miami center so they would be expecting us flying in to clear customs and enter the U.S.

The weather was good until we got near Andros Island which is one of the larger Bahamas islands just south of Miami. It was getting dark and I could see lightning; that meant thunderstorms. At night you can see them better because of the lightning. So you can try to navigate around them. Never fly into one. They will tear a small plane to pieces. I encountered a lot of heavy rain and some turbulence, but not too bad. The passengers were a little nervous at this point; I assured them we could go around the storms with no problem. As we got closer to Miami I tried to contact Miami center to get clearance to enter the ADIZ (air defense identification zone) and clearance into Miami. This is an imaginary line around the United States going out about fifty miles covered by military radar. When an aircraft enters this zone headed toward the U.S. they must contact whatever radar center covers that area. If they have no contact a Customs plane would be sent to intercept you. If you are flying in excess of 400 knots it would be a military fighter or they might track you in and see that you clear customs on landing.

The radios were getting a lot of static and I couldn't hear anyone talking. They were old radios with tubes and not solid state; I think they were getting wet from the heavy rain. I noticed the generator hand was showing a discharge so I had a short circuit somewhere, probably something getting wet. I started cutting the radios off and on, then the navigation lights, trying to find out what was causing the short. Now I was in Miami airspace about halfway between Miami and the Bahamas Island of Bimini which is about fifty miles east of Miami. I had not been able to contact Miami radar to identify me but I knew they must have seen me on radar. There was a large thunderstorm between me and Miami and landing there was out of the question. I flew on up the coast trying to find a hole in between the storms where I could go inland and land. I still had not been able to contact Miami control for radar coverage. I finally got one radio working and could hear other airplanes. By now I was up the coast past Miami near West Palm Beach. I saw a break in the storms and turned inland to look for an airport to land so we could clear customs. We were somewhere over Lake Okeechobee just south of Orlando. I managed to contact Orlando approach. I was still getting a discharge on the generator needle and I cut some more lights off and on. I cut the strobe on the tail off because it pulls a lot of amps. That didn't solve the short problem so I cut it back on and Orlando looked clear.

Finally, I got clearance to land. We landed with no problem. The passengers and I were relieved. While taxiing in to the parking ramp I saw flashing yellow construction lights on the taxiway that was under repair. I was trying to get around them when the control tower told me to stop right there and shut the engines down, that some people wanted me out of the airplane. I looked outside now and we were surrounded by people with weapons pointed at us. We got out of the plane and were ordered to put our hands up. This was the DEA. They had been following us in because we had not contacted Miami for clearance to enter the U.S. ADIZ zone. We had been picked up on Miami radar and hadn't reported in.

We were searched and two agents started searching the plane for drugs. They couldn't find any in the plane or the bags. The DEA guy in charge seemed upset because he was sure we were trying to sneak into the U.S. without being seen since I had cut my lights off. I had to go take a leak and the pilot of the chase plane went with me; he seemed like a nice guy. We got inside and he laughed and said the guy in charge was so pissed we had no drugs on board. Miami had scrambled their plane and a jet to track us. He said when I cut off the strobe light on the tail they couldn't see me; they flew within thirty feet of my tail to keep me in sight because it was so dark and I had all the lights off trying to find just what was shorting out in the electrical system. When I cut the strobe light back on, which is about the size of a coke bottle, it flashed into his eyes and he couldn't see a thing. This light can be seen for at least ten miles away and he was blinded. He pulled up so he wouldn't run into us. He grinned and said, "Thank goodness there was another pilot on board that could fly the plane." It was a Beachcraft King Air. I told him I had filed a flight plan but I didn't know if was transmitted or not. He didn't know.

When we walked back out to the plane I saw that they had taken off all the inspection plates and had an Orlando police dog sniffing each hole and inside the plane. It was starting to get comical as this guy in charge couldn't find anything other than we entered the country without notice. I told him I filed a flight plan for Miami. He finally let me make a phone call to my wife. She told me she got a call from the coast guard in Miami that they had received my flight plan but the weather was so bad in that area that I probably didn't try to come in; they figured I had landed in the Bahamas somewhere. That told me they had received my flight plan. I told the guy in charge but he was still acting like an ass; he did say he would check it out. We were cleared to go so I fueled up and we left for Nashville. They finally let us go. It was late when we got to Nashville and I spent the night there and left for Louisville the next morning.

About two weeks later I received a letter from the customs & immigration dept saying I had entered the country illegally and was to pay a fine of $1500. I then got a letter from the coast guard in Miami stating that I had filed a flight plan and they were notified we were in route for the U.S.. I sent a copy of the letter back to customs and told them my flight was legal and I had not committed a violation of airspace nor entered the country illegally. I strongly objected to the outrageous fine. About two weeks later I got another letter reducing the fine to $100. They just wouldn't admit they were wrong. My attorney said, pay the $100 and let it go. I took his advice, still sure it went into my record.

While having lunch a couple of days later I got a call from one of the local flying services. They had a guy interested in a charter. He was planning a trip to Jamaica and I was recommended to him by one of the flying services at the airport. They did not fly out of the U.S. Also none of their pilots had the experience I did. He was flying down commercial and wanted me to meet him and two others in Montego Bay, Jamaica. They wanted to look over some property they were thinking of buying. Later that day the guy called me back said his name was Frank Biggs. He wanted to meet me and go down with me. The other two were coming back with me and him with maybe a stop in the Bahamas or Florida.

So about a week later I prepared to leave. I did not have a six place twin at the time; mine was on lease to a flying service, so I had to lease one from a friend. This was a Piper Aztec like I had before and I liked those planes. All my planes were always for sale or lease. So if I got an offer I couldn't refuse, it was gone and I would be in the market for another one.

At this time fuel in the Caribbean was scarce. It was in the late or mid 70s. A lot of the islands did not have any fuel as many of the domestic oil companies were on strike. I knew I would only need four of the six seats in the plane so I took out the last seat. It was a bench type seat in the rear of the cabin. I set two fifteen gallon plastic containers in its place. I fueled up the plane, the tanks and the two containers. A few nosey people saw me and the rumors started, again, that I might be smuggling dope.

I wanted the extra thirty gallons as a back up. They would give me about an hour and ten minutes of flying time over and above the normal five hours of standard fuel load. If course I would have to land somewhere and pour it in myself. I called Biggs and he said he would get a commercial flight and meet me there.

So I left for Florida, stopping at Albany, Georgia to refuel, then on to Ft. Lauderdale, Florida then nonstop to Great Inagua Island in the Bahamas. This is the southern most island in the Bahamas chain. Just off the Cuban coast. The airstrip looked deserted. I thought I had enough fuel to proceed to Jamaica but just to be on the safe side I would put in the extra fuel I had in the containers. While doing this another plane landed. It was a nice twin larger than my plane. The pilot was from Grand Cayman island and was on his way back home. He also wanted fuel. He said he circled the town twice; that was the signal to send someone out to the airport. The town was very small with only ten to twelve buildings.

The only industry at great Inagua is Morton salt. They have salt pits all over the island; they pump sea water into them and it evaporates and leaves salt, sea salt as pure as you can get.

After about fifteen minutes two islanders showed up and unlocked the fuel pumps and we topped off our tanks. They questioned the two containers I had in my plane. I told them it was a back up if I landed somewhere and no fuel was available. They informed me they were one of the few islands in the Bahamas, including Aruba and a few others, that had fuel. Shell fuel only as they were a Dutch company and not a U.S. company.

Skip was the name of the other pilot. I filled out the necessary forms, paid for the fuel and left for Kingston, Jamaica. We flew together. He knew of a good hotel where we spent the night. I got up early the next morning, had breakfast with Skip, said goodbye and took off for Montego Bay. This was at the other end of the island.

After landing I called the hotel where Biggs was staying. Took a cab to the hotel and met with Biggs and his two friends. You ever have a gut feeling that something is not right? I had that feeling. But I was committed to the flight so I tried not to think about it. I should have listened to my gut instinct.

Later that day after lunch they wanted to fly over some property about eight to ten miles from town. It was a good looking beach area and a high hill top overlooking a golf course with a beautiful view of the sea. This was my second trip to Jamaica and I have to admit it is a beautiful island. Jamaica's largest industry is mining bauxite, a prime ingredient in aluminum. They have a year round growing season for their second industry, marijuana. It grows everywhere. Little kids would try to sell it to you on the street.

After about two more days of flying around now they wanted to drive back to some of the locations we had flown over. I had been warned not to go with the locals unless you knew them. Biggs knew that one Jamaican we met there was on something. He just acted like it. He seemed nervous he also had a pistol; he said it was protection. I didn't go with them. I stayed at the motel and enjoyed the pool, beach and sun.

After they returned Biggs told me we could leave in the morning and his other two friends would be flying back commercial.

I got up early the next morning and I filed a flight plan direct from Montego Bay to Miami, Florida. No problem on fuel. With my two containers full I knew I could make it without stopping. I had to clear various departments, airport security, customs and immigration. Each one has a fee. Of course a $20 bill dropped in the hand of a customs man would speed up your clearance. After about an hour of running here and there we were through. I had told Biggs I would meet him by the plane which was parked quite a ways down the ramp from the main terminal. I still needed to top off the fuel tanks. It was very hot by now. It was almost noon in July with virtually no breeze. As I walked up, he was waiting with our bags by the plane. By now, sweat was rolling off me. I opened the nose baggage door and put the bags away. I checked the oil and wondered where the fuel truck was.

I got up on the wing to open the cabin door to let the hot air out of the plane. I squinted into the plane and saw black plastic bags about a foot square where the two plastic containers had been. Then the smell hit me: marijuana.

I turned to Biggs and asked, "What's going on?" He smiled and said it would be no problem and we could drop it off in Miami. I felt my blood begin to boil hotter than the Jamaican sun above us. I said, "Get that crap off my plane." I told him we would never clear customs. He said it would be dark when we got to Florida, to just go in low under the radar; he knew of a small airport where we could land and unload. I wasn't convinced. He said he would make it worth my while and offered me $15,000. I refused. He then raised it to $20,000. I told him we couldn't just land at these small airports in Florida after dark. If we did the local police would be there to check us out five minutes after landing on the ground.

By now security was wondering why we had not gotten into the plane and departed. I saw two uniformed Jamaicans walking down the ramp toward the plane. I told him I did not want these guys near the plane with the pot in it. I still needed fuel so I walked up to meet them and had another $20 in my hand and told them I needed a fuel truck. One called on his radio and suddenly a truck came out of nowhere and started down to the plane. They turned and walked the other way. Thank goodness.

After fueling the airplane two little Jamaican boys came out to the plane wanting Biggs to pay them for the pot. I told them to unload it-- now. They wanted to cut the price; Biggs still wanted to do the deal. He was upset; I insisted. Security was now headed back down the ramp to see what the hold up was. I went up and met them and said we would depart soon as I finished my preflight. They didn't have time to unload the pot. Trash compacters were a big seller in Jamaica and the islands. They used them to compact Marijuana in black trash bags into a forty pound square block. This was what I had on board.

We departed at once with about 300 lbs of pot on board. I did not want to get caught with it. Even the smell can put you in a Jamaican jail forever, unless you have enough money to pay them off.

We flew past a beautiful resort with people lying on the beach. It's an absolutely beautiful island. On board, things weren't so pretty. We were still arguing about what to do with the pot. I was not going to chance flying it into the U.S. Biggs said he should have said something earlier but this was a spur-of-the-moment opportunity to take it back. I said we could drop it off in great Inagua, remembering how deserted it was. He could make other arrangements to get it to the U.S. I was now headed down the Florida straits between Haiti and Cuba. I came in the same way on the way down to great Inagua Island in the Bahamas. Leaving Jamaica behind, we are now just south of Guantanamo Bay, Cuba. I took a reading off their radio beacon, a VOR to you pilots, to check my position. I could see Cuba and the tip of Haiti. Choosing to fly closer to Haiti than Cuba I started a slow descent to about 800 feet above the water. Descending above water is tricky. I had no reference points such as trees, houses or even boats to judge heights so I hoped my altimeter was set at the correct barometric pressure setting. I had heard of pilots flying right into the water because they couldn't tell how high they were above the water. I came in low with the engines throttled back. I didn't want to attract attention.

The runway on the island is 5000 feet long running north and south. I touched down and taxied up toward the back side of the parking ramp. Here Biggs jumped out to off load the pot in the tall grass and bushes there. Then we planned to take off and head for Miami.

He had just finished when I turned the plane around, looking up to see an old yellow ford driving fast in our direction Biggs was still outside when they rolled up; three Bahamians rolled out with guns in hand pointed in our direction. I was tempted to takeoff and leave him because this pot deal was his idea in the first place. But, being the good guy that I am, I shut the engines down and got out. If I had it to do over again he would still be standing there and me airborne. They ran up to the plane and we put up our hands. Their heavy weapons were a rusty snub nose 32 cal pistol and a single shot 410 shotgun. The guy that appeared to be in charge came up. He looked in the plane. Then he smiled. He ordered me to get out of the plane and come with them. Apparently they saw Biggs unload the pot. We were taken to the local police station. It was a small wooden building in town. We were charged with importation of drugs and entering the country illegally. We were never searched, just asked for our identification. Then we were taken to jail. The jail was a sight to see. It was out of the 1700s, built to hold refugees from Haiti. I would guess it was about 150 to 200 years old. The glass imbedded in the top of the walls was smooth from the weather over the years. The thick walls and interior was a stucco type about foot thick. The four cells inside had dirt floors, no electricity and large heavy wooden doors on the cells, and a canvas folding army cot in the cells; they put us in separate cells.

About 5 pm they unlocked the door and took us to a large colonial-type home like you would find on an old Southern plantation. It had a porch wrapping around most of the house. It was a three-story house. They took us inside and fed us one of the best fried chicken dinners with mashed potatoes, pinto beans and biscuits that would melt in your mouth. I couldn't believe it. After we ate we were taken back to the cell. It was getting dark now. There were no blankets or pillows so I just laid on the cot. After awhile, I stood up on the cot and grabbed hold of the bars in the window. They were rusted. I began twisting them back and forth; soon they started coming apart. I realized I could easily get them apart, climb out and get over the wall. I also realized that I was on an island. How would I get away? I decided to stick it out. I had some matches and found some small sticks on the floor. There was a busted up army cot in my cell so I used some of the wood and sticks and started a small fire. I could hear things crawling around while I lay on the cot and I hoped the fire would deter them from getting too close. Fortunately, I still had my Swiss army knife; I cut up more wood and kept the fire going for a while. The dry wood made virtually no smoke. I finally dozed off and slept through the night.

The next morning we were given a large cup of coffee and bacon & egg sandwiches. So far the food was good and we had been treated well. After breakfast we were taken before a magistrate and charged with possession of drugs and entering the country illegally, not importation. The magistrate had a white wig on like you might see worn by government officials in England. The courtroom was small. We were asked to plead guilty to possession; if we did, we would be fined $1500 and charged was a misdemeanor. We would be released for immediate deportation from the Bahamas. We jumped at this. I couldn't wait to get off this island. Our money, which had been confiscated earlier was returned and Biggs paid the fine. They then told us the airplane had been confiscated because I wasn't the owner. It would be held for a price. It seemed that all they were interested in was money. Now how were we going to get off the island and get back to the United States? I thought other planes needing fuel should be landing soon and maybe we could catch a ride to the U.S.

We started walking toward the airport and a Bahamian woman and a young boy gave us a ride in an old 1957 caddy. The boy told us the authorities had their own thing going by selling pot to certain people that fly in and pick it up. He said the jail was full of it. Also, as I suspected, he confirmed they worked with smugglers for fuel. That was why they had arrested us; we hadn't paid them off.

We arrived at the airport. The airplane was tied down and I noticed it had a flat tire. They had let the air out of the left tire so we couldn't take it. After checking further I saw they had taken the battery out and the radio compass. This was a radio to tune in low frequency navigation beacons in the Caribbean. If I had the tire pumped up and a battery I wouldn't need the radio; there was enough fuel to make Florida. Just head 330 degrees heading and you can't miss Miami. Or just follow the island chain up.

We didn't have to wait long. After about 25 minutes an old Beachcraft Queen Air landed. The pilots, one of which was Cuban, didn't seem to know much about flying. They agreed to give us a ride to the States. They put fuel in one side of the plane. We loaded up. There were no seats in the plane except the pilot and copilot seats up front. We sat on the floor and I asked what they had been hauling. He said they took some tractor parts down to Colombia. There were extra fuel tank hookups in the rear of the plane. Some smugglers used waterbeds for fuel tanks lying in the back of the planes; hook up a pump and they'd be in business. They were headed for Miami.

After about an hour I heard them talking and they seemed excited about something. I asked if there was a problem. The Cuban said they put the fuel in the wrong side of the plane. It was a twin engine plane. I told them to turn on the cross feed and transfer it to the other engine. He said the cross feed on that side didn't work. Great. Here we were with one dumb pilot and an el stupido. I asked the Cuban if he could fly the plane on one engine; he didn't know. I told him to get in the copilot seat and I would fly the plane. I had about 25 hours in that type of plane and I was checked out on single engine procedure. I calculated the time and distance and figured we could make Nassau, Bahamas before we ran out of gas in the right engine. So I headed for Nassau. It was closer than Miami. We still had both engines running when we arrived in the traffic pattern in Nassau and were cleared to land. While taxiing to the parking space one engine quit, out of gas.

So dumb and dumber refueled both tanks this time and we left for the U.S. and landed at West Palm Beach, Florida. We cleared customs and Biggs and I took a commercial flight back to Louisville, Ky. We hardly spoke on the way back.

CHAPTER NINE

Stealing the Plane

Now I had another problem. I had left a friend's airplane sitting in the Bahamas. He was not a happy camper when I told him. These Bahamians are known for seizing an aircraft for some reason and holding it for ransom. The Great Inagua airport had four or five airplanes sitting around looking like they had been there for some time. If they thought they could make a deal they would take the planes to Nassau so they could lock it in a hanger and hold it for a ransom. We had to get this plane out of there before they moved it. I had another friend who owned a security service. I had the idea of going down and taking the plane. I called Pete and he was all for it. He had a twin engine six place plane and he would take two of his guys with a couple automatic weapons and grab the plane. Pete liked the idea just for the thrill of it. He just wanted expenses to do it.

We decided to do it the next night. It would be a full moon; in the islands it is bright as day with a full moon. We loaded up with two men, me and Pete. We got to the island about 10 pm. He came in low with the engines pulled back as I had instructed. He landed and rolled up next to the plane. We all jumped out. The two guards were instructed to fire over the head of anyone that showed up. One had an air tank and pumped up the tire while I put the battery in. I also had one of the guys put in about ten gallons of gas from a can we brought, just in case. I untied the plane and jumped in while Pete taxied out of the way. I started both engines. His guys jumped in with him and we were off. We had been on the ground only four to five minutes.

I knew I had enough fuel to make Miami. It was a smooth flight and we talked on the radio some and commented on how beautiful the moon looked on the water. A couple of hours later we arrived in the Miami area. We both landed and cleared customs. The Bahamians would never say anything because their activity was illegal. We fueled up and headed for Louisville.

The next morning Pete and I met for coffee. He had loved the trip. We called Biggs and told him the cost and he was glad to pay the expenses. The going rate to get a plane back from them was generally between $25-30,000 for the Bahamas customs. That was the last contact I had with Biggs and that was fine with me.

CHAPTER TEN

Selling to a Drug Dealer

I advertised the Aztec in a national trade paper for aircraft and was getting a few good calls on it. One day I got a call from a man who said he was from eastern Kentucky. He wanted to meet with me and have his pilot look at the airplane. We set a date and met for lunch. He had his pilot with him and later the pilot and I went to the airport to look the plane over and test flight. The buyer's name was Randy Garner. He told me he had come by the airport earlier to look at another plane and wanted to look at mine also.

He wanted his pilot to fly the plane and we took a 20-minute check-out ride. This guy wasn't the sharpest knife in the drawer. He was very nervous and wasn't sure of himself as a pilot. He said he had a lot of hours but didn't certainly didn't fly like it. I thought maybe he got his hours as a passenger. But his boss wanted the plane and I didn't much care how good he was as long as I had my money.

A few days later Garner called and wanted to meet and discuss price. We did and agreed on a price of $71,950. Garner wanted additional fuel capacity added to the airplane. The model Piper made after this model had extra fuel capacity added. I didn't want to go to the extra expense of having this done without a substantial deposit to cover the modification. At this time he had not given me any money. I agreed but the mod change would cost about $8,000. Randy said he would pay for the tank installation. I had someone to fly the plane down and come back on a commercial airline. Randy came up with the money and I paid the pilot to take it down. After about a week I got a call that it was ready. I went down to pick it up. It was in Florida, all legit, with proper paperwork.

Randy then wanted his pilot to fly it for a day or two to get familiar with the plane. I told him no way unless I had full payment for the plane. I didn't trust his pilot; besides, if he crashed it, I would be out of an airplane. Randy didn't have as much in the deal to lose at that point. He agreed to give me half to let his pilot fly it. I said no. He said he would come up with the balance in a week or two. I suspected what he intended to do was to fly the plane to out of the country to bring back a load of pot and sell it to pay me. If he did that and his pilot got busted, I could lose the plane. It sat for about ten days and we met again when he had the balance of the money. All cash. The first payment was a casher's check and on my cash deposits I did them in $4,900 each so no one asked any questions about the money.

I was now in the market for another plane more suitable for hauling patients. One I could get stretchers inside with ease. I did locate a piper Seneca in Tennessee. That was a really nice plane and very well equipped with radios and autopilot. And it was in my price range. It worked well with one stretcher inside and it could accommodate two if need be. Most of the flights were with only one stretcher. I always had a paramedic who went along. I made a few air flights with patients and it worked just fine. I did lease the plane out to a flying service when I wasn't using it.

I was contacted by a local guy who wanted me to do some flying for him and a few more people. Told him my rate and he wanted to go the next week to Jamaica. "Why?" I asked. He said to look at some land for sale. The same as Biggs. I wasn't too happy with it but the pay was good.

I had heard of this guy. He had a reputation of dealing in drugs. His name was Jim Allen. I ask him again of his intentions to ensure we were not going to bring back pot on the plane. He it was a legit flight. He even had his own airplane. He had just purchased a Piper Aztec twin engine and it looked to be a nice airplane.

We left Louisville two days later in his airplane and landed in Miami, Florida. I refueled and headed the same route as before. Flying down toward the tip of Cuba, turning west through the Florida Straits between Haiti and Gitmo. We landed at Montego Bay late that day. He had his own room and I had mine. We met for dinner and two Jamaicans joined us. They planned to meet in the morning; I would stay at the motel. It was a very nice Holiday Inn. It had a nice pool and was near the beach. I was happy to let them go. Jim said they would be back by lunch time.

I enjoyed the beach and the pool while they were gone. They came back in a couple of hours and we all had lunch. They wanted to drive down the beach and asked me to go with them. We went about ten miles and I noticed white poles about every fifty yards on each side of the road. I asked about them; they were put there by the government to prevent smugglers' planes from landing on the road. We finally got to where we turned in to go to the beach area. It was a nice secluded beach. No houses. We got out and Jim asked me if a plane could land on the beach and take off. Right then I knew exactly what this trip was for. I looked at it and judged the length of the beach, hard sand, to be about 2,800 feet with trees at both ends. I told him yes, I could land and take off, depending on the plane and how heavy the load was. So I asked him up front what the load would be and what kind of plane. He had his plane in mind and had a pilot. He asked if I would be interested. I wasn't.

The next morning we prepared to leave. I filed a flight plan and we took off. He asked to fly near the beach area where we were yesterday. As I approached about a mile out he asked if I would land and take off right away. A touch and go so to speak. I said, "Sure, what the heck?" I turned in and dropped the gear, chopped the power, landed, came to a complete stop. He was surprised I did and I taxied back, full power and took off, cleared the trees with no problem. He was all smiles at this point. I then said we were not loaded so it was not a problem. He then said he would make me a great deal if I would fly for him. I just shook my head no.

We got back to Miami a few hours later, cleared customs and they checked the plane with a dog. I must have been in their computer from the Biggs' deal. We were clean.

We had dinner and left for Louisville. He said he had another plane he had just purchased and I could fly it for him. It was a Cessna-210 single engine, a nice plane and fast. I had owned one before.

He called me two days later and wanted to meet for lunch. We did and he then made me an offer to fly because his pilot didn't have the experience I did. He didn't trust his flying ability to do this job. I had just proven you could land on the Jamaican beach and take back off. After thinking it over, I decided his offer was just too good. I could use the money; my charter business had been slow. I don't know why I kept thinking I would just do this one last trip and quit. I knew how to get into the U.S. without being detected and had done it a few times. We would use his plane and I wouldn't put mine in harm's way. I was pretty sure I could get in under the radar like before. But it was still risky.

We left two days later and flew to Montego Bay Jamaica after a stop in Miami, Florida. I refueled the plane and got it ready for the next day. This plane had long range fuel tanks so fuel would not be a problem. We spent the night and met the same two men from the first time. They would have people ready to load the plane as soon as we landed. We wanted to leave later in the afternoon so it would be late and dark when we entered the coastal area of the U.S. I had flown in the U.S. from the gulf area at night before on other trips and just didn't want to land and go through customs. I had flown low over the water and never had a problem before. I figured I would try the same thing again. This would be impossible today as the coastal areas are watched with satellite, every plane leaving anywhere south of the U.S. borders.

We left about 2 pm and in a few minutes I saw the beach area. I turned in, dropped the gear as before and landed. I turned around and four men came running up to the plane. Jim jumped out and opened the cargo door. We had the Cessna with long range fuel tanks he had just purchased. They loaded the plane in about four minutes, waved me ok and Jim jumped in. Off we went. The take off was slower this time and I saw the trees at the far end getting bigger and bigger. There was a good breeze coming in off the water. I held it on as long as I could to get more flying speed. I pulled up at the last minute and barely cleared the trees. My gear, while coming up, brushed the tree tops. I was up and turning out to sea before I realized how close I had been. Jim was happy and smiling. He said his other pilot would not have made it. I said, "Hold that smile until we're safely home."

The plan was to fly into the everglade area of Florida. He planned to drop the pot off in a field to some people on the ground. We would call them on a radio channel they had set up. Then we would look for a spotlight shining up. That would be the drop zone. We flew about 5 hours from take off and up past Bimini, Bahamas. I dropped down to about fifty feet above the water, turning inbound and paying close attention to my altitude. When flying over water, it is hard to judge altitude and it is impossible at night. I got my altimeter setting from the Miami airport. I just didn't tell them where I was. There were no lights for reference and I, of course, had my navigation lights out. By now my hands were getting sweaty and concentration was a must. My heart was pounding fast. Suddenly a light appeared right in front and close. There was light fog over the water. I almost didn't see the light.

I pulled up and went right over a large ship. *God, that was close.* Had I not pulled up I would have hit the mast. I was lower than I thought. I reset my altimeter and stayed at fifty feet. Jim started to say something but I cut him off. "Don't talk to me. I need concentration."

Now I saw coastal lights and relaxed a bit. Just as we passed over the coast suddenly there was another light in front, a strobe. I realized it was closer and a high power line. I dropped down and flew under it. This was getting sticky to say the least. By now I was sure my armpits were wet. Jim wasn't saying anything. Maybe he was too scared. We were headed for alligator alley. I eased up a few feet and picked up the car traffic lights and followed them west. Then alligator alley was the only straight highway across Florida. There was a blinking light about halfway; that is where we turned south. A few minutes later I spotted the blinking yellow light. I turned south and Jim was on the radio. I saw a spotlight shining up ahead about a mile or two away. I cut back the power and dropped down a bit. They had headlights on and were parked in a road running north and south. He then told me that there had been a change of plans. The area was clear of wires and had been checked out and used before. He wanted me to land on the road just past the first car. The people on the ground would meet us to unload.

The moon was out now and the road was clear. I didn't turn on my landing lights until I was about tree top level. The moon was full and the road was straight and long. I landed and rolled to a stop. As I was breathing a sigh of relief, two trucks rolled up and three people and Jim started to unload and were done in about four to five minutes. He jumped back in and shut the door. I shoved the throttle forward and took off headed for the Tampa airport on Florida's west coast. Jim crawled in the back and picked up a plastic sheet we had spread over the back so to catch any fallout of pot. He then installed two seats we had folded up in the back. We landed at Tampa to refuel. We went in to relieve ourselves and when we got back out to the plane two DEA agents were waiting for us. They had checked the plane out and wanted our ID. They made a note of who we were and thanked us and left. I got a fuel truck and refueled the plane. Glad they didn't have a dog to sniff the plane; it would have smelled the pot. I was tired and I wanted to get out of the area. I checked the weather and we headed for Louisville.

Al Isley

CHAPTER ELEVEN

Run for Jim Allen

Jim called me the next day and asked me to come over to his house. When I got there he handed me a bag of cash. He said it was what he promised me for this last run. I didn't count it at the time. I did count it when I got home. There was $25,000. He said he might want another run in a week or two if I wanted to go. I still had not told my wife what I had just done. I did tell her I was paid well for the charter.

I didn't mention the twenty five thousand. I hid most of it in a small safe I had in the closet. Only I had the key. I paid off the car and a few more bills.

Jim said he was thinking about another trip but no more beach landings. We would be going to Mexico. I hesitated and he upped the offer to $35,000. It was hard to resist this kind of money. He said while there I might be able to go to Columbia. Some people there wanted to fly back to Belize; I would be paid on the spot. So I told the wife I had some more trips to make and she didn't ask too many questions.

A few days went by and Jim called me again. He wanted another run. I called him back and we met for lunch the next day to discuss the trip. He wanted just me and him to go to Belize and stay there for a day or two while he made contact with people there. He was excited for this could make him a lot of money and he would have an opportunity to meet some major people in the business. In the back of my mind I was thinking this would probably be my last trip if we had no problems. Belize is on the west side of Mexico Yucatan peninsula. It has a reef that's great for skin diving and second to the Great Barrier Reef in Australia. But he wasn't going for skin diving. Back then, there were not nice hotels and resorts. Now, it's a big vacation spot.

After this I figured I should have enough money that I could stick to regular charters and not take anymore risks. I considered myself lucky so far. Just missing that ship was pure luck. That scared me. Avoiding accidents and not getting caught. I was getting deeper into this than I had planned. And I didn't want my luck to run out. God must have been watching over me for a reason.

Jim said he was buying another airplane and wanted me to go check it out and fly it around for a day or two to get used to it. It was in Columbus, Indiana. I went up, got it and flew it for a day or two. It was a nice airplane. It was another single engine Cessna 210. He had sold the one we had just flown. It was always a good idea to get rid of a plane once it is used for a smuggling run. The number could be hot. The government tracks plane numbers when they go in and out of the U.S. frequently.

The new purchase was a really nice airplane. He had his mechanic take out the rear seats. They were bench type seats. This plane had long range fuel tanks installed. Having good radios is a must along with a good engine for the type of flying he wanted to do.

We left the next day for Mobile, Alabama. There we refueled and headed over the Gulf toward Mexico and flew directly over Mexico to the Belize City airport. Belize is on the west side of the Mexican

Yucatan Peninsula. Belize City airport and the country at that time were protected by the British and had Harrier Jets stationed there. When any plane landed, there was a rocket pod mounted about halfway down the runway just off to one side in a bunker. It tracked each plane down the runway. This just made me a little uneasy to say the least. But we cleared their customs and there were two people waiting for us. Back then there were no nice hotels. Just a few old rooming houses where you could rent rooms. They had a private home rented down the beach about twenty-five miles. There was a landing strip there about 2800 feet long. The house was right on the beach. It was old but nice, a colonial style home. A small restaurant was across the road. Lobster at two dollars a plate. Jim met privately with the two guys and I enjoyed the beach till dusk. Then the "no see-ums" came out, little small flies that bite. I hurried back in the house for a beer.

This is where we were supposed to pick up the marijuana and go back to the U.S. This is where I met Jim's cartel contact Danny and I picked up his cocaine in Columbia and then flew it to the U.S.

CHAPTER TWELVE

Newsflash!

It had been about two weeks since I sold my plane, the Piper Aztec, to Garner. I had forgotten about getting back in touch with Jim until I was watching the eleven o'clock news that night and they reported that a Piper Aztec was seized at the Louisville airport that day. It was registered to Jake Thomas of the ten thousand block of Cherry Hill Rd in Louisville. *ME*! That SOB Garner never changed the registration. I hate to say it, part of this was my fault for not sending it in myself. They went on to say that I was not being charged. Well, this was a shock to say the least after what I had just been through. Mentally I was beat and this was a hard blow. My wife didn't hear the newscast and I didn't say anything to her. I called Garner. He was upset; he had tried to call me earlier in the afternoon when he heard. He was pissed and thought I had something to do with it. I knew I hadn't but thinking back I tried to put some things together.

About ten days before he bought the plane I had rented it to a pilot whom I had known around the airport for some time. That was not unusual. I rented the plane out to pilots I knew that met the requirements for insurance.

This pilot met the time and ratings for the insurance. No problem. I had flown with him and I was satisfied he was a safe pilot. His name was Jack Bell. Jack's brother Tom had a reputation of being involved with drugs. He also bought and sold airplanes, flyable and wrecks. Tom owned and operated an aircraft junkyard and salvage company in Indiana. Jack and Tom had rented the plane early in March of this year and flew to Texas to look at an airplane; they returned the next day. I had never known Jack to be involved with any drugs so I wasn't worried. But I later found out that they took one other person with a large sum of money with them for a drug deal. We found out later that's the reason the plane was seized.

So now Garner was out of a plane. He asked if I would locate him another plane like the one he just lost, but not as expensive. I started checking the Internet and trade papers. The next day I was at the airport and I got a phone call. It was the DEA. They wanted me to come down to their office and talk about the plane I sold Garner and asked if I had a bill of sale. I told them I did but they still wanted me to come down around 2 pm. I didn't want to go. I called an attorney I knew and he advised me not to go without him. He said he would call them and we could meet in his office which was only a block from theirs. They were pissed, he said, and wouldn't come down. He also said that I wasn't being charged. So I forgot about it for awhile.

Later that day Garner called and said he had gotten his plane back. Apparently he had his copy of the bill of sale for the plane and they gave it back to him. He still wanted another plane anyway; I located one in Ohio. A dealer up there had one advertised that sounded like a pretty nice plane. I flew up and looked at it and the plane had been well cared for, just high time on the engines but they ran good and they were good for another two hundred hours before overhaul. I called Garner and he said he had looked at one in Louisville that was for sale, a local plane. He gave me the tail number and I knew it right away. It was the one I flew to Jamaica, the one that had gotten seized in the Bahamas. The one I had to go get. The price on it was more than the one in Ohio so he opted for the Ohio plane. I cut a deal with the dealer and flew it back to Bowman field in Louisville. I had a local shop do some work on the plane and give it a new inspection. We put better radios in it for I knew what he wanted to use it for. I told him the maintenance cost would be about five thousand and he was fine with that. It actually was twenty eight hundred so I did ok on the deal.

During the next few weeks I didn't hear from him and I had a few charters. He called in late March and said he was having some radio problems with the one I sold him. I recommended a shop in Muncie, Indiana. The airplane I purchased in Tennessee was also up there so I told him to have his pilot fly us both up and ride back in mine as it was ready. After arriving in Muncie with his pilot flying I was glad I got my money before I let this guy fly my plane. He had not improved.

I hadn't heard from Jim and I assumed he had found another pilot or just wasn't doing anything. Jack's brother, Tom, had the aircraft salvage yard in Indiana. He didn't fly much and in the past he had me fly him around to different places from time to time to look at aircraft for sale. He called and wanted me to fly him to Jamaica to look at a couple of aircraft. I told him up front, okay, but just the two of us would be coming back, nothing else. We left the next day. I had trouble convincing the wife this was a legal trip. Not to worry. We took a plane he owned, a nice twin that he wasn't qualified in. I had all the proper paperwork for customs in both the U.S. and Jamaica. We flew to Miami, Florida, refueled and headed south around Cuba to Kingston, Jamaica. I was getting to know this route pretty well now.

After landing we checked in at the Holiday Inn and had dinner. He got on the phone with someone and asked for them to meet him in his room. I was in the room when someone knocked on the door. I opened it. Two Jamaican policemen were there. They asked for permission to come in. I thought, "Oh, shit, we are busted for something." Tom came in off the patio and they introduced themselves to us as his contacts. They had two planes in a hanger at the airport and also they worked drug contacts. They could load you up in the hanger and everything was cool until take off. I looked at Paul and he said, "Not this trip." He was interested in the airplanes only for now. I figured he must have known about these guys from other contacts.

At the airport the next morning we looked at the planes. They were okay to me. I could tell they had been sitting for a while. One twin engine and one single. I told him I would stick with the single and leave the twin alone. So he cut a deal with these guys and said he would have a pilot fly down commercial to fly it back. I really didn't want to fly either of them back. I was a little leery of not having a good inspection on it before flying over a lot of water. Plus the plane numbers could be hot and get stopped by customs and I didn't need that. We left the next day and had a long boring flight back to Miami, cleared customs and then Louisville.

About two days later Jack called and said he had a friend that had to get to Houston, Texas the next day and asked if I would I fly him down. He would pay cash. This was a spur of the moment thing and he couldn't get a commercial flight direct to Houston. I didn't have a plane available. Mine was on lease to someone in Ohio. I said I would try to find one I could use. I did know of a Piper Cherokee six that a friend owned. It was a six passenger single with a large 300 hp engine. Nice plane. I had leased from him before. He kept it in a T-hanger there on Bowman field in Louisville. I called Jack and told him to have the person meet me at the airport at eight o'clock the next morning. I met Jack and the man in the flight office on the field. The passenger was a man in his 60's, well-dressed with a nice crop of gray hair. Very pleasant. I gave him a price to get him to Houston later that day. He was okay with that so I filed a flight plan and his only luggage was a nice leather carry-on type bag. I started to put it in the nose baggage compartment and he said no, he would just keep it with him. He wanted to sit in the rear seat. This plane had six seats. Two front for the pilot and co-pilot and two center seats and two in the rear. He got in and sat in the rear seat.

We took off and headed for Biloxi, Mississippi. This was a refuel stop. I looked back at him later and he was asleep. A little over three hours later I was close to Biloxi. Time to wake this guy up. I shook the plane, yelled at him but he didn't stir. I put the plane on autopilot and crawled back and grabbed his foot that was lying on the center seat and shook it. Still, he didn't move. Now I was getting worried that he might have died. Right there on the plane. I was now just a few miles from the airport so I crawled back and turned the autopilot off and called the Biloxi control tower for landing. I didn't say anything about this guy to them yet. I got in the traffic pattern; on my final approach I felt a punch on the back. He was awake—and alive!

We landed and while I refueled he made some phone calls. He called me over and asked how much more to go to Brownsville, Texas. Brownsville is on the border of Mexico and Texas. Change of plans. So I went inside and checked the map and gave him a price; he agreed to it. Now I was wondering why the sudden change, but, I was getting a good price for the charter. It was late when we got to Brownsville, just after midnight. The control tower was closed and he called a cab and said he had two rooms at the Holiday Inn so I could spend the night. We got to the motel and went to his room and he opened the leather bag. Now I knew why he had been so attached to it; he brought out a wad of cash. He counted out my money and gave me a key to the other room. After saying goodnight, I went to my room and called the wife. I told her where I was spending the night and that I planned to leave the next morning. I'd be home in the afternoon.

The next morning I got up early and went to the coffee shop for breakfast. While eating, in comes my passenger. He wasn't alone. With him was a Mexican-looking dude with a thin mustache, open shirt and gold hanging around his neck. They didn't notice me and sat on the other side. I started to put two and two together with the bag of cash and Brownsville, Texas and this Mexican. I figured it was a drug deal. But my deal was that I was going back alone. I got the motel to take me out to the airport and refueled the plane. I filed for Memphis, Tennessee for a fuel stop. I went by Biloxi coming down due to weather in Tennessee. I got back that afternoon in Louisville and put the plane back in the T-hanger. The owner of the plane generally leaves the key hidden in the door of the hanger so I put it there. I left him a check in the glove box of the plane for the rental of the plane.

The next morning I got a call from Wayne, the airplane owner, saying the Feds just called him and asked if he was flying his plane yesterday. He told them no, that he had leased it to me for a charter. So they called me shortly after that and wanted to talk. I called the attorney and he presented the same deal, his office not theirs. They didn't like it but we met anyway. They, the Feds, liked to record everything without your knowledge. They were really interested in the guy I took to Brownsville, Texas. I told them he originally wanted to go to Houston but changed while we were in Biloxi. They said he had pretended he wanted to go to Houston because they knew he was meeting someone in Brownsville. They were watching the airport. They saw us get out of the plane; they took down the tail number and found out who owned the plane, Wayne. I don't remember the passenger's name now but they wanted to know what name he gave me then. The bag had over $600,000 in cash in it. No wonder he didn't let it out of his sight. The Feds said he was going down for a drug buy. They wanted to know how he chose me to fly him down. I told them I was referred by Jack Bell. They had a few more questions but the attorney told me not to answer them; they smiled, thanked us and left.

About a week later a large four engine DC-4 plane landed at Bowman Field in Louisville at night after the tower had closed and was left there for a few days. The airport operator had someone climb up into it to check it out. No one had contacted him about leaving it there. It had been parked there for about a week. It was a large airplane and took up a lot of space. The line boy that climbed up to check it out. He said there were marijuana scraps all over the floor. So they called the DEA and they came down and wouldn't let anyone go inside the plane. A witness said when they parked the plane that night he saw two men get out and meet someone in the parking lot in a car and drove off. They probably unloaded the pot somewhere else and this plane was a throw away. They used it just for the run and left it in Louisville to take the pressure off of wherever they made the delivery. Found out a few days later the plane had landed in Lexington, Kentucky and off loaded over twenty thousand pounds of marijuana. Who got it, I never found out; it was the drug buy made from the guy I took to Brownsville. Lexington, Kentucky was becoming a hub for drugs. It was in the newspapers and talk around the airport also. My information sources then were pretty good.

Lexington, Kentucky was said to be hot in drug dealing; rumor had it the local police were involved along with some local politicians and prominent families. A Lexington DEA agent had gone into the drug business for himself and was sought after by the FBI. Drew Thornton. Later he was flying in a load of cocaine when he and his partner spotted another airplane tailing them. They started to dump the bags out with parachutes and let them float to the ground over Tennessee. He and his partner bailed out over Knoxville. He had about a hundred pounds of coke hanging to him and his chute either couldn't carry the weight or it didn't open as it should. He was killed on impact. A guy came out early the next morning to pick up his newspaper and saw a body in his driveway. It was Thornton. He had been on the FBI's wanted list for some time. He was from a prominent family in the Lexington area. His family had a horse breeding farm and was far from being poor. An old Kentucky family from old money. Guess he just liked the thrill of it all.

The DEA agent that was checking the DC-4 airplane that landed in Louisville was Harold Brown. I heard that he was involved with this plane load of pot. A short time later he was shot and killed in his apartment in Louisville. The local newspaper said it was suicide. Two men were seen leaving his apartment that night. A local pilot from Lexington was rumored to have been one of the pilots that flew the DC-4 into Louisville. I heard it had about ten tons of pot on board that they off loaded in Lexington. Witnesses had a habit of disappearing in some of these drug cases. They discovered a female floating in the Kentucky river before Thornton was killed near a large piece of property on the river that Thornton owned. It was a dangerous business.

CHAPTER THIRTEEN

DEA Set up

Remember when Jack and his brother rented my plane and flew it to Texas before I sold it to Garner? Well, they took some people with them that had cash for a drug buy. About ten days later two people drove a large truck back loaded with marijuana. This was a set up by the DEA. The drivers were DEA agents. They were trying to get the local dealer. A lot of drugs were coming into Kentucky and Indiana. Jack and Tom were some of the people they were after but they had to catch them with or buying the drugs. But luck was with Jack and Tom; they didn't meet the truck. They had three other people meet it and direct it to a farm out in the county and, I guess, stacked it in a barn. So the DEA decided to call in backup and busted the three. However, they now knew where the stash place was located.

Now Jack and Tom were indicted on a warrant out of Texas for their alleged involvement in this conspiracy. They made a few trips back and forth to Texas on hearings. Finally it was time for the trial. Jack was acquitted and his brother got six months of weekends at the county jail. After that things were quiet for a while. And I was thinking I had better get out. I knew too many people in the business and I was along with them. I had imported a lot without thinking about it. I didn't use it or sell it. I had just been lucky not getting caught.

A couple weeks later there was a knock at my door. It was Jim and a female; they wanted to talk. I told them to leave and not to ever come to my house. I would meet them somewhere else. We met at a local restaurant. The women was from New Mexico. Her name was Helena. She was a big drug dealer in the west and Midwest. She was looking for a pilot and Jim suggested me. How he had gotten to know her I don't know, but word gets around in the circle. She wanted me to do a run from Mexico to Texas. She had a plane but her pilot had gotten drunk, tried to sell some pot, gotten busted and was in jail in Houston, Texas. She had already paid for the load and it was setting in Mexico. She was desperate to get it out and to Texas. She said she had about 400lbs of it stashed there.

I wanted to talk to Jim and we excused ourselves and went outside. I didn't know this woman and didn't know if she was trustworthy, She could have been working for the DEA. He said she was big in the west and she had good connections. It would be a favor to him if I could help her out.

We went back inside and I agreed to do it, but only once. I told her I wanted $40,000 plus expenses to make the run. She offered to pay $20,000. I said, "Forget it." I had been lucky before and I really didn't need to do it. Jim stayed out of it and she came up to $30,000. It would only take two days. One day down and one day back. Unload, spend the night and fly back home. I said I would do it if I could have the money up front. Somehow I just didn't trust her.

She went to a phone booth and made some calls. I heard her speaking Spanish so now I knew she was fluent in both English and Spanish. I learned later she was from Germany originally. She was all business. She said she would give the money to Jim and I could collect it when I got back from Texas. I now began to realize what I was becoming: one of the large importers of drugs for Kentucky. I knew I was not the only pilot doing this but I knew I was doing my share. I've always hated being put on the spot like this. I really wanted out of the business. However the money was good and I had paid a lot of bills off. I am thankful that none of my kids used drugs, neither did my wife nor me. Today, it is worse for kids than it was then. Crack and speed weren't around then like it is now.

So I committed to do this run. Until now, I had never come in on the west coast to the U.S. Now I had no oil rigs to fly close to and this was an unproven entry point. *Here I am taking another chance that I shouldn't be taking.* Helena had a plane in Bardstown, Kentucky I was to use. It had never been used for smuggling and was not hot. When the DEA suspected a plane was being used to smuggle drugs, they would tag the plane number and watch it. Sometimes they would plant a bug or transmitter in it and follow it in. Control towers had a hot sheet with airplane numbers on them provided by the DEA to check when a plane on the list lands at the airport. They then would report the plane's location to the FEDS.

The plane I planned to fly would be fine, at least that's what I was told. I went down and checked it out. I turned on the battery switch to see if it had a tracking device on it somewhere. I had a receiver that would pick up the tracking signal being transmitted after the battery switch was turned on. I had been to Bardstown many times as it was only about forty miles from Louisville. It is a pretty town with some nice restaurants. Stephen Foster's home was there. There was a small three bedroom inn on the main square and it was rumored that Jessie James had spent the night there and shot two holes in the wall. The holes are still there.

The plane looked good and had long range tanks on it. I flew it back to Louisville. Helena, Jim and I met for lunch and discussed where I would land in Mexico and Texas. It was determined I would take off in the morning and check out the landing spot in Texas near Corpus Christi. But first I would meet Helena in Ruidoso, New Mexico.

I left the next morning and flew direct to Ruidoso. It's located in the mountains and is a very pretty area. I checked into the Holiday Inn for the night. It snowed lightly overnight and the next morning the ground was white. I sat in the coffee shop and watched the snow evaporate. There was no humidity and it didn't melt; it just evaporated. Meteorologists call that sublimation; the fallen snow goes from a solid state to vapor without going to liquid.

Helena called and said we would meet the next morning. I just hung around for the day. When we met, she had a young guy with her. He didn't talk much and after breakfast we went to the airport and all three of us left for Victoria, Texas. It is located just southeast of San Antonio. After we landed she made a phone call and about twenty minutes later two more people showed up. One of them was a Mexican-looking dude with shifty eyes and a distrustful look. This must have been her contact from Mexico.

They didn't trust me because they didn't know me and had expected the other pilot. For all they knew, I could have been a FED. She assured them I came recommended. They still wanted to search me to make sure I was not wearing a wire. After they patted me down and were satisfied I was okay we discussed where I was going to land.

We then got in their car and drove about fifteen miles out of town on a long straight country road. It was a nice blacktop road with electric or phone wires on one side and some brush on the other. The wires and poles were no problem; they were far enough off the road for the wings not to hit. There were no cross wires on the long strip of road which was about 4000 feet long. Plenty of room for a landing and take off in the twin engine Piper Aztec. At takeoff the plane would be empty and low on fuel so there shouldn't be a problem with weight. The cloud cover hopefully would be high if there was any. The weather looked good. I was to call a certain radio frequency when about 15 miles out and then again when I was about a mile out and they would cut on a light to shine up to guide me in. Then headlights would light the road at each end of the landing area. So this end looked good if I had no problem coming in through the Adiz Zone. Helena was going with me to show me where to land in Mexico. It was on a large ranch and the owner had everyone paid off so there would not be a problem landing. It was a private strip about 3000 feet long with no trees in the way.

We both left the next morning. She had a couple of bags to take along. It was just the two of us. After a couple of hours flying down the coast, she told me to head for Tampico, Mexico. It sits near the Gulf so we would stay near the water. She was watching the coastline carefully. Then she told me to turn inland and about 5 or 6 miles inland I spotted the landing strip. They even had a windsock so you could tell which way the wind was blowing. We landed and two trucks drove out to meet us. Helena spoke to them in Spanish. She got out the two bags she had loaded in the plane. She opened one of them and handed out pistols to these guys. I didn't like this but she said they needed them for protection. Some of the others already had weapons.

Four Mexicans drove up in two trucks that held the pot we were to bring back. They started to load it and another truck came up with 55 gallon drums of gasoline for the plane. They had a hand pump and filled all the tanks with fuel. It didn't take long; obviously they had done this before. Soon we were ready to leave. It was a relaxed atmosphere, seemed no one was in a hurry. I had a jug of water, some fruit and we weren't on the ground but about an hour. I was ready to get going back.

The distance was not as far as the Jamaica or Belize run had been. This was only about a 5-hour run and all up the coast. She said she was not going back and one of the guys, Pedro, who was helping with the loading, would be going with me. He told me in English he was from San Antonio, Texas. So we got in and took off and I turned up the coast.

It would still be daylight when we would be coming into the U.S. I planned on staying out to sea for about 70 miles and then turning in toward the King Ranch in Texas. This is the largest ranch in the U.S. Lots of coast line. And not populated. After about three hours I turned inbound and dropped down to just under 100 feet. I was using the same method I used before on the east coast. Pedro was getting a little nervous that close to the water. I had been monitoring Corpus Christi radio and getting altimeter settings. When you're that low it's very hard to judge your height above the water.

I started to pick up land just ahead and then a ship, probably Coast Guard, off my two o'clock position. I did not want them to see me. The sun was setting and at my nine o'clock so if they were looking toward my position they would be looking into the sun and couldn't see me. I dropped down lower, so low the prop tips started picking up spray on the windshield and Pedro really got excited. He was yelling and I pulled up a few feet. I was really low.

I came in right over Padre Island. Stayed low, just under 100 feet and flew inland for about 30 miles and turned north. The land there is flat and there is a lot of desert. There was a small airport off to my left a few miles and I then started to climb up to about 5000 feet. I then headed north for Victoria, Texas. Pedro was more relaxed now that I had climbed up to a higher altitude. It was getting dark and in another hour we would be there.

Things were going through my mind and I wished this was all over. I was determined that I was going to end it when I get back home. I had heard of guys who made a lot of money and then retired. Up to this point, I had not gotten caught and my record was clear. After this, I would just continue my regular charter business.

I was 15 miles out when Pedro made the radio call. Got a quick answer and that's all. A couple of minutes later I called again and I spotted a light shining up off to my right. I headed for it. The light went out and Pedro spotted the headlights on the road. I dropped down to 1000 feet and circled around. I chopped the power for a quick descent. I touched down and was rolling to a stop when the left wing hit something. A road sign. Someone had failed to remove it during the day. They had put out detour signs on each end of the road intersections just before dark with flashing lights. These people were good at their job, except for the guy that was supposed to remove the sign post.

They started off loading right away. Pedro was out and helping. It only took about 4 minutes. While they were off loading I jumped out and looked at the damage to the wing. There was a small gash in the leading edge of the wing, not bad. Also Pedro was yelling at one of them that he was supposed to have removed the sign. I told them to get that sign removed now. I told them to hurry up so I could take off. They could kill each other later; I could care less. I didn't want a car driving down the road while I was preparing to take off.

The sign was removed and I started both engines. I took off quick because I was not loaded. Pedro stayed there and I headed for Austin, Texas about 45 minutes away to refuel. I landed at Austin and taxied to a parking area not too close to the terminal. I walked in and ordered a gas truck. I asked if they had any silver duct tape. The guy behind the counter gave me a roll and said to use all I needed. I went back out and taped up the hole in the wing. A lot of us pilots call it 200-mile-an-hour tape. It's great stuff.

When the gas truck showed up, I refueled, gave the tape back and departed for Shreveport, Louisiana. I spent the night there in a Holiday Inn. Seems I always wind up in one. I didn't want to stay in the area and have the plane number near where I refueled or landed on the road. I called the wife and said I was in Louisiana and would be heading home in the morning.

I got up the next morning and left for Louisville, or rather Bardstown, Kentucky. The weather looked good all the way. There was no control tower in Bardstown so the plane number wouldn't be shown. I called Jim and he came out and picked me up. He was interested to know how everything went. I went over everything and he said to come out to his house the next day and he would pay me. I got in my car and went home. Believe me, I was tired.

Jim called me the next day and we planned to meet for breakfast. He said to come over to his house. Helena had given him the money when she was there. She didn't want to pay me up front in case I got caught and she had no product. Product is what they call the drugs. Jim insisted she give him my money. Jim wanted to know when I would be ready for another run. I told him I was pushing my luck now and just didn't want to consider doing it again. "Consider me retired." He said pilots like me were hard to find. Many got caught on either their first or second run. The government was cracking down much more than they had in the past. They had more money than in the past for more agents and equipment. I told him I would be in touch. For now I just wanted to do my charter business. Period.

I wanted another airplane just for personal use and started looking around for one. Our family would like to take another vacation after school was out for the summer. We planned to take a friend and his wife with us to Mexico. The wife and I with our son had been down twice. If you know where to go you can have a nice time and it isn't too expensive. Mexico City has one of the largest museums in the country. It takes about two to three days to go through it. We also considered visiting the islands.

I didn't want any more visits from the Feds. I knew I was on their list because each time I would come back through customs, me and the plane were checked.

I did locate another airplane and flew to Knoxville, Tennessee to look at it. A nice twin engine Piper Seneca. We were in the office discussing price and in walks Tom from Louisville. He was buying a wrecked plane there and wanted to talk to me about another flight. Going to Mexico, he had heard of the one I had just made. I refused his offer. How did he know this so soon? It worried me because if he knew it so soon the Feds might also know about it. I told the aircraft owner I would be in touch and left for Louisville. I did not want to buy another plane and look like I had plenty of money to spend if the Feds had heard about the Texas deal. I made some charters for the next few weeks and didn't hear any more about it.

We with our friends did take a Mexican vacation and were gone about ten days. We had a great time and hit a lot of small airports in Mexico where the airlines don't land. These towns were not tourist spoiled. We saw quite a few ruins and took some great videos.

I was anxious to get back to work and make sure my son, who had stayed behind with friends, was okay. And, of course, when we came through customs at New Orleans the airplane and our baggage were checked. And my name was run through the computer. I told our friends this was normal now with so much smuggling going on whenever you come in the U.S. from another country.

We were all happy to get home. Our kids were fine. They'd had a break from parents for a while but were glad to see us. We could hardly wait to get our many pictures developed. It had been a good sightseeing trip.

CHAPTER FOURTEEN

The Indictment

I should have invested the money I had made the year before. I really didn't know how or what to do with it. In my spare time I coached and refereed soccer. My son loved the game and was a very good soccer player. At this time he was ten to twelve years old. We had a travel team and tryouts to make the team were a must. We had kids from all different school districts. In school season they played for their own schools and played against each other. Off season they were a great team and we traveled to other states and played other select teams. This went on up through high school. We even took five teams of five age groups, ten-year-olds through eighteen-year-olds to France one year. What a great trip that was. Most of the parents went and a good time was had by everyone. We flew to Brussels, Belgium and were met by people with Mercedes buses. This had been arranged by the soccer club with some visiting French delegates visiting Louisville the year before. The French have a national soccer tournament each year and a lot of European countries are invited; our kids got to play different country teams. I was one of the coaches for the ten-year-olds; they did great and came in third place. The twelve-year-olds took second place. The French were amazed that we Americans could play soccer so well. Something our kids will remember all their lives. My son is now thirty-eight and still plays in a men's league.

In the spring of 1984 I received a visit by the DEA at my home one afternoon. Two agents came by and wanted me to take a ride with them in their car. I didn't; we stood in the driveway and talked. I knew one of them; he was a soccer coach and my team had played against his team. My daughter drove up with a girlfriend and she asked me later who those two guys were; she thought they looked like hoodlums. Somehow the Feds thought I was involved with someone dealing drugs. Either Garner or Jack's brother Tom had used my name in some conversation and it was showing up a lot. They knew about the Texas case, the guy I flew down with money for a drug buy. Then I sold a plane to Garner, a drug dealer. He had used it to bring in a load of marijuana; by this time they had run a check on me in their great computer in the sky and found out about the Biggs' deal in the Bahamas. They found out I had plead guilty to drug possession there. I couldn't be charged for that in the U.S. as it was in another country. They thought I knew more than I made out like I did and could give them more information on all the local dealers and importers.

Now they were not as nice as before. They started with threats. "Tell us what you know or we will indict you." And "If you don't cooperate, you will do time." They had their minds made up; I could be a witness for them. They finally left and said they would be in touch.

So now I was on their list of suspects. One afternoon in October 1984 they came to the door again, same thing, same conversation, same threats. Then in November they showed up a third time with a warrant for my arrest naming me in the Texas conspiracy with a trumped up charge to pressure me. One agent started to handcuff me and the one

I knew stopped him and said no, it was okay. I was taken downtown and booked in the Jefferson County Jail in Louisville.

I was supposed to go to a certain cell block with other inmates and was changed to a private cell. I wasn't put in with other inmates. Then the person in charge of the jail and all bookings came by the cell. He was another soccer coach I knew and saw my name come in on the booking sheet. I had not known where he worked; he changed my cell. He said I wouldn't have wanted to go in the mix with some of the other inmates. There were a lot of bad guys in there. I thanked him for that. His name was Rick. I don't know if he still there or not. This jail was about 70 or 80 years old. Louisville now has a nice modern jail. But this one was something out of the Stone Age.

I spent about ten days there in my lonely cell before my attorney could obtain bond. My wife brought me books to read and I did get some rest. The U.S. Attorney set my bond at a ridiculous amount of $100,000. I finally made the 10% to get out. The food was typical jail food: a baloney sandwich and weak tea or coffee. Nothing like the fried chicken we got in the Bahamas jail.

About a week or two later my attorney said the DEA and Assistant U.S. Attorney wanted to talk to me. Just like the last time, they had no evidence, as we found out later, just someone saying I could have been involved in something. If they arrested certain people they wanted me to testify against them. I didn't know anyone by the names they gave and I had never had any association with them. They still weren't convinced of that. So more threats were made. Such as, they would indict me again if I didn't cooperate. I kept telling them I didn't know these people and they didn't know me. After about an hour we broke up and left.

I went back to flying and heard nothing for the next six months. In March of 1985 another indictment came out naming 31 people on it and I was one of them. I called my attorney and went down and surrendered, but at this time there was no warrant issued, Just a summons. I was booked and fingerprinted as before but no jail time. I was ordered a bond of $20,000. Then changed it to an O/R bond, "Own Recognizance." A couple of weeks later my attorney called. The charges were the same as before. They had no evidence but threats of another indictment if I didn't talk to them. They somehow were convinced I could hand them a big case with a lot of the people. There were 31 names. I just didn't know all these people, Only Jim, Jack and his brother Tom. I wasn't talking and they weren't happy. I think they had busted some guy selling and he threw my name out; my name was hot by the aircraft sales and the Bahamas' deal. They had no evidence of my flights bringing in any drugs. So I continued my charter business as usual.

About six months later another indictment with about 30 names on this one came out. Of course I was on it. It was interesting that all those indictments had the same names, same group of people on them. An Assistant U.S. Attorney went to the Grand Jury and they came up with a lot of different stories; the Grand Jury didn't know any difference. The Assistant U.S. Attorney convinced a DEA agent to testify before them. He had quiet a story and came down with an indictment. A person in this position can really abuse his power. And in this case it was for personal gain. This was a big case and he was hoping to get an appointment as the U.S. Attorney for the western district or possibly a Federal Judgeship that was coming up. By the way, he got neither; he was passed over for both jobs. He just wasn't well liked by people and other attorneys as well.

In the last or third indictment we didn't even have to ask for bond. The U.S. recommended another O/R bond.

Remember the first indictment that got me jail time? Well, one other person was named on it, Jim. He must have gotten word the indictment was coming down and left for parts unknown. Later we found out he had fled to Mexico. He was missing for over a year. The DEA dug up his yard with a backhoe the day after I was arrested. They were looking for money or drugs they heard Jim had hidden in the yard. Someone had told them he had money and drugs buried in his yard. Well, this turned up nothing more than news on the TV and in the newspaper. Unfortunately I was the only one arrested and they pictured me on the front page of the newspaper being led out of the courthouse. Jim was caught over a year later in Mexico and taken to Los Angeles for a week or so then brought to Louisville for trail. No bond for him.

After a number of hearings the U.S. wanted to try the second indictment first. The first one on me was a throw away anyway. It was a conspiracy charge on the Texas case to say that I conspired in the Western District of Kentucky. It was just BS to get an indictment. The second one had 31 people on it. Their chief witness was Garner, the guy I had sold the plane to. He had been busted in the spring of 1985 and was out on bond. While out on bond he was busted again for possession. His pilot had set him up having turned informant.

Al Isley

CHAPTER FIFTEEN

The Trial

The trial started in March of 1986 and Garner was put on the stand as the first witness for the U.S. For the first eight to ten days of the trial Garner testified. He told of how he started in the 60's using and selling marijuana. He said he had used or tried just about everything on the market. He said he drove marijuana from Florida in the 70's and early 80's for Jim then decided to go into business for himself. He even admitted giving his children marijuana when they were ten to twelve years old. This guy was something else. He testified that he would rather have them smoke pot at home than on the street.

In the late 70's he was also buying drugs locally and trying to start an import business. He and Jim had an open agreement that Jim would get half of what he brought in and he would get half of any Jim brought in to sell.

After a few days more of testimonies, other people took the stand. During their testimonies my attorney would ask if they knew me; none of them did. Finally it was my turn. Up to that point, I had not been called to the stand. Garner said on direct examination by the Assistant U.S. Attorney that he did not know me until he purchased a plane from me. Also I wouldn't let him have the plane until he paid in full. And I didn't trust his pilot. He said he didn't tell me what the plane was to be used for until later after he bought it. He testified that he asked me to fly for him and I refused. My attorney crossed examined him briefly, then we broke for lunch.

During the lunch break I asked my attorney why was I still here. There was no evidence on me. He said he would get into that on cross examination with Garner.

When we came back from lunch the Assistant U.S. Attorney started a re-direct on Garner, covering how he had paid for the airplane. We objected because my attorney hadn't opened any doors in that area but the judge overruled us. He then changed his story and said he provided me a down payment and I agreed to let him fly in a load of marijuana before paying me the balance. He was a government witness and over lunch they determined to strengthen his testimony in saying I had financed the plane for him. This was an out-and-out lie to make me look more involved. Somehow, during lunch, the government had gotten him to change his previous testimony.

As I said before this was a man I didn't even like, but he was a buyer for my airplane. I didn't know him from a load of coal, so I would never let him, or his pilot, fly off in my airplane when he had not paid me for it. It would be stupid to do a deal like that. No one would. He could have flown off and I would never have seen him again. I didn't even know where he lived. The U.S. had two aircraft dealers they called in. When asked by my attorney if they would they agree to a deal like that, they said no way, that it was ridiculous to even ask that. And this was the U.S. witness. The U.S. attorney didn't like their answer on that. They weren't helping his case and they were dismissed.

The deal was this: Garner paid me money to have long range fuel tanks installed and I furnished the pilot to fly it to Florida to have the work done. I still would not let his pilot have the plane until I was paid in full.

He continued to testify for a few more days on the other defendants. My attorney asked each one if they knew me. They didn't. The only testimony against me was Randy Garner at this point, saying I had financed the plane for him. They were supposed to have another witness to testify against me but he had disappeared. I don't know what his testimony would have been. I didn't know any of these people except Garner and Jim; and Jim was nowhere to be found.

This trial went on for two and a half months, only stopping for a few days off and on for the trial Judge to check up on the law. As I said before, he was a newly appointed Judge and had been a tax attorney before the appointment. This was his first case. He was not versed in the law in this field and would stop and read up on it. In my opinion, he would have been a better tax Judge.

The U.S. had run through most of their defendants except one; they brought him in at the last minute. His name was Paul and he said he could identify me. He said he was one of the people who unloaded the cocaine from the plane when I landed in Kentucky. I did not recognize him and he couldn't have me either. He must have been promised a deal by the U.S. Attorney to say he knew me. He was busted trying to sell some pot and he got no time later for his testimony. I stayed in the plane on that unload and didn't get out so he couldn't have seen my face. I wore sunglasses and a ball cap. The government case against me was very weak; they wanted a conviction on me because they thought I was a major player in the drug trade in Kentucky and Indiana. Actually there were no drugs ever shown or seized in the trial. The whole trial was based solely on testimony. I had brought in a lot of marijuana and the one load of cocaine but there was no evidence against me for that; there was just testimony from people who were busted for selling drugs that didn't even know me. We broke for the day and the Judge said the defense could plead their case the next day.

All the attorneys pleaded their case. By now, after two and a half months, the jury was tired and confused. They were mostly all older; some retired. One kept falling asleep and was replaced. By the time it was all over they couldn't remember who testified against whom.

Finally, after two days of deliberation, the jury came back. The verdict was guilty, for all of us. I was shocked. I was convicted on a conspiracy charge. In other words, by selling the airplane to Garner who had used it to smuggle drugs, I had been made me a part of the conspiracy even though I didn't fly the plane for him. By the same token if I had bought a car for a bank robbery with someone else and I backed out of the deal and didn't participate in the robbery I wouldn't be in the conspiracy. It applied only to the drug trade.

I was taken into custody at once with the others and put in the Jefferson County Jail. The first night I was in the drunk tank. Glad it wasn't a weekend. There were only two drunks in there. I, and most of the others from the trial, had dressed in suit and ties for court; they took our ties and shoe strings. We slept on the floor that night. I didn't get a lot of sleep. Sometime during the night they brought in a couple more drunks before morning.

The next morning we were processed and put into individual cells. I spent three days in a separate cell then was taken to a jail about fifty miles from Louisville, The Bullitt County Jail in Elizabethtown, Kentucky. This was a holdover jail the Feds used until the federal prisoners were turned over to the BOP (Bureau of Prisons). I spent six weeks there. This was also a maximum security lock down jail. I was mixed in with all types of prisoners, the good the bad and the ugly but only about four people to a cell. There were murderers, bank robbers and general jail birds. One thing I learned in the Air Force, in this type of environment you keep your mouth shut, do what you are told. Be polite to those in charge and don't trust anyone around you until you get to know what's going on. Then keep your guard up. Don't get into long conversations with anyone; just keep to yourself so you don't attract attention.

I never saw so much illiteracy in my life than I did at the county jail. Most federal crimes were a higher class of crime and inmates went as high as congressmen, lawyers and judges and so on. Most of the other defendants went somewhere else or were kept in Louisville at the Jefferson county jail. Only about four of us were sent to Bullitt county jail.

The first two days here we spent in the mix of prisoners and then transferred upstairs to the federal cells. By law they could not mix federal and local or state prisoners together. My first day here one of the prisoners in an adjoining cell had loaned his Bible to a prisoner in my cell and wanted it back. He said it belonged to his wife and had a picture of her in it. This guy said no, he wasn't through with it. The other guy really got upset and started screaming and cursing and the jailer had to quiet him down. I later asked the jailer why he was so upset, his wife probably wouldn't mind sending another picture. This guy said he was in jail for killing his wife. He had strangled her with a rope. I didn't ask any more questions.

Later I was put upstairs in a two-man cell. The other inmate there was a pretty friendly guy. He told me to take the bottom bunk, that he preferred the top. He said he would be transferred out soon anyway. I didn't know what he was in for; that is something you just don't ask. He left a few days later and the jailer told me he was a serial killer. He had killed five people. He was back in Kentucky to stand trial about a girl he killed when he was only fifteen years old. He had tied her to a tree and ran a car into her because she wouldn't date him. I never saw him after that day and later read in the Louisville paper that he had been convicted and sentenced to life.

I was in jail about six weeks and my wife and son came down faithfully every Sunday to visit. Also a lot of friends came down; they said I got screwed as there was no evidence on me. The guy that lied to get a deal from the U.S. because he was busted trying to sell pot got no charges.

Through all this, my wife was fantastic. She now had to support herself and our son. He was still in high school, a freshman, and teenagers go through clothes and eat like there is no tomorrow. I was really proud of him; he was a great soccer player and athlete. I had a little money but not a lot from all I had been paid. My attorney fee was over $50,000. I felt like I had thrown that money in the street; it didn't do me any good. Fortunately, my wife would get the $10,000 back soon for my bond. Being apart from my family made me realize what a large part of my life they were; I missed them very much. My daughter had left home a couple years ago and was married and living in Phoenix, Arizona.

This jail was a lot cleaner and the food was much better than the Louisville jail. These jailers were all from the same family and were just good "old country folks." The lady that cooked for the jail was the cook at the Holiday Inn and she prepared some good meals for us.

We did have a day room with a ping pong table and a weight machine. I played ping pong daily. We had a TV and that took up some of the time. There was a library next door where we could check out books to read.

At this time, the reason I hadn't been turned over to the BOP was that I had two other indictments; I had hearings to attend at the federal courthouse in Louisville. The U.S. Marshal Service would pick me up to take me to Louisville for my hearings and some of the others on the indictments. At this time I hadn't been sentenced.

CHAPTER SIXTEEN

Guilty

I was found guilty by the Jury in May of 1987. The Judge didn't sentence me until July 30 of that year. One of the reasons there were so many discrepancies in my pre-sentence report that had to be corrected. He also noted that my only involvement was in selling an airplane to Garner.

At my sentencing my attorney resigned from the case. I was shocked. We had talked of him appealing my conviction. My wife and I had signed an agreement to put a second mortgage on our house for a guarantee of money for the appeal. I later learned that as soon as I was found guilty he walked down the hall and registered a lien on the house. This house didn't have a lot of equity in it. We sold our other house in order to pay him and the fine. He was charging us $500 an hour. Some days we were only in court about two hours or less, some days more. So you can see his bill was high. This last house was in my wife's name because I couldn't get a loan with all the indictments on me.

Now I didn't even have an attorney to file an appeal. One of the other federal prisoners was pretty well versed in criminal law. He suggested I file the appeal myself. We call these guys, Jailhouse Lawyers. He was pretty good and we made many trips to the law library next door. We did a lot of research on double jeopardy. I then filed a double jeopardy motion for the other two indictments. They were clearly double jeopardy as the time frames ran inside the one I stood convicted on. It was the same district, the same statues and same defendants. I was appointed three different attorneys by the court, none of which would do anything. They all wanted me to plead to the indictments. One of them was to do my appeal and then I found out he was about to be disbarred. So I filed the motion after I got all of them dismissed and was appointed a good attorney.

When you can't afford an attorney the court appoints one. Guess who pays the attorney? The government. The same people who are prosecuting you. The Judge asked me who wrote the motion and I told him I did. He commented it was a better motion than a lot of the attorneys he had before him. He asked if I was a lawyer. I told him no, that I had just done a lot of research in the county law library. That appeared to impress him. He said he wished some of the lawyers would spend more time in the law library.

My new attorney came highly recommended and was hard working; he wasn't afraid to go head-to-head with the U.S. Attorneys office. He didn't like the Assistant U.S. Attorney and welcomed the case. I signed a waiver to wave any further court appearances by me, letting him handle it. So after twelve months, my stay there was not that bad. Most of the time I had a single cell and the head jailer and I got along great. They didn't even lock my cell and I would go downstairs and have coffee with the other jailers. There was a small passageway behind the cells. When problems arose with the plumbing, I acted as plumber and took a tool box behind the cells and fixed a lot of the problems. Also when I needed a haircut, they would give me four dollars and send me down the street to get a haircut.

I was outside one day getting some cigarettes for the jailer out of the trunk of his car. Two DEA agents drove up that knew me and came unglued. They started raising hell with the jailer that I was outside with no escort plus I had the keys to his car. The jailer told them in no uncertain terms that this was his jail and he would run it how he wanted to. They then shut up and we all had coffee.

They finally put a cell mate in my cell. He had gotten into a fight with another inmate in their cell of four. My cell was located at the far end of the cellblock and no other cells were near me. It was pretty quiet. He was a young kid from Texas. He and another guy had been persuaded to making speed. He was the cooker. The undercover DEA pretended to be a buyer and convinced him and a buddy to go into the drug business and they (the DEA) even provided them with the items to set up the lab to cook the drugs. They told them to come to Kentucky and they would set it up for them. The DEA had sent a guy down there to get someone to set up a lab in Kentucky. Their informant spread some money around and these guys were in debt and saw an opportunity so they moved to Kentucky. The feds even gave them money for expenses. The one guy with me was married and his wife stayed in Texas for the time being. The DEA had a drug lab set up for them somewhere in the county with all the necessary equipment. They started making the drugs on Friday and were busted on Monday.

His name was Pete. There was another empty cell beside mine and they moved him in there. We talked a lot for the first few days; he was worried about his wife. He had used drugs for the past few years. He was hooked pretty bad and had needle marks on both arms and ankles. I felt sorry for him. He called home about one to two times a day. When he did get to talk to his wife they would argue. The phone was on the wall next to my cell. He found out someone was sleeping with his wife and that made matters worse.

One day about 10:30am he called home, talked to her and hung up. He was angry and went to his cell. I was writing at the time and he hung a blanket in front of his cell. This was common as the light in the hall shined in his cell and he couldn't sleep. I saw him moving around in there and about 11:30am the jailer brought lunch by. Pete yelled out that he didn't want any. I ate and went back to writing. About 1:30pm I took a nap and he was still up then. About 3:30pm I got up to watch TV till about 4pm. The jail shift changes at 4pm and a new jailer comes on duty to make his rounds checking each cell. He asked if Pete was asleep; I said "probably" and he left. I walked out of my cell, stood in front of his cell and couldn't see him. I called his name he didn't answer me. I pulled the blanket down. I couldn't believe it. Pete had hung himself.

I called downstairs to the jailers on the phone. One came running up, unlocked the cell but wouldn't go in. I ran in and checked his pulse. He was cold, stiff and pale. The one jailer wouldn't go in to get him down. He called another jailer; there were only two on duty. He and I went in, took him down and put him on the floor. They called the Feds and they showed up with the coroner. The coroner said Pete had been dead for over three hours.

Pete left a suicide note. It began by stating where to send his body in Texas and then revealed pressure put on him by the U.S. Attorney's office. They wanted him to go to Texas and set up more people so they could be arrested. He had a letter from one of the Assistant U.S. Attorneys in Louisville threatening him with sixty years in prison and a $2,000,000 fine if he didn't co-operate. The pressure was just too much for the poor guy. I read the letter and the suicide note before the U.S. Marshals got there. He had torn a piece of sheet and used it to tie around a vent on the back of his cell. Stood on the toilet, tied the end around his neck and stepped off. I don't think I will ever forget that picture of him hanging there as I looked in to check on him.

About seven months after I was convicted in December of 1987, Garner testified in a hearing for double jeopardy in the third indictment. He said he had borrowed $75,000 for the purpose of buying an airplane. He borrowed the money from Jim Allen, my co-defendant in the trial. He stated he didn't borrow all the money at one time but a couple of days apart. He then stated Jim was paid back the $75,000 plus an additional $75,000 out of the proceeds of the sale, making a total of $150,000 payback to Jim. No mention was made that any of the proceeds were to go to me to pay the balance of his claimed indebtedness at the previous trial, showing I did not finance the airplane for him. We filed for a new trial. It was denied.

I realized that this Judge wasn't going to admit he screwed up. His big mistake was listening to the Assistant U.S. Attorney who was prosecuting the case. It wouldn't look good if they admitted their chief witness was a liar. Garner was testifying to suit the case or whatever the prosecutor wanted him to say. We played the tape in the trial where Garner was talking to his pilot and his pilot was wired with a recorder. Quote: *"I will lie, cheat, steal and do anything to stay out of jail."* As of this writing, he is running a jewelry business in Lexington, Kentucky. He has never been sentenced.

Also brought out in the trial was the gross misconduct of the U.S. Attorney's office. Garner's pilot, the informant, had a load of marijuana on the plane, stopped in Atlanta, Georgia and called the DEA. They came out and did nothing but told him to continue doing what he was doing. All they wanted him to do was to let them know when he was leaving and coming back. He made three or four trips that we know of down and back hauling drugs each time and getting paid $30,000 each trip. He was landing near Lexington, Kentucky near Garner's farm and no one ever showed up to bust anyone or seize the drugs. He asked them what he should do with the money and they told him to keep it. Now here was a guy running drugs with the sanction of the DEA. A perfect set up. He was arrested briefly in Jamaica, but all it took was a call to the DEA and he was released. He wasn't even on the indictment as an unindicted co-conspirator. He then said his current job was flying for UPS.

Al Isley

CHAPTER SEVENTEEN

Going to Prison

After the trial was over and my appeals exhausted I was moved to a Federal Correctional Institution or (FCI) in Lexington, Kentucky. This used to be a drug hospital and was a very large facility. It was fenced in and covered a lot of ground. I was only sixty miles from home and also surprised to hear no more men were to be shipped here. The FCI was co-ed. Men and women convicted with light crimes.

On the way over the two marshals transporting me and a woman stopped at a McDonalds for lunch. They bought us Big Mac's and cokes. Nice guys. They had my handcuffs so lose I pulled my hands out to eat. One of the marshals said, "Don't forget to put them back before we go in the FCI."

After we checked in an inmate escorted me to my dorm. They didn't have cells here, just dorm rooms. This was in June and the weather was warm. We walked outside and I couldn't believe my eyes. There were gorgeous women sunbathing in shorts and bikinis. What a trip. I was holding my blankets and sheets and almost dropped them, stumbling and staring. The guy laughed and said I would get used to it. Looked like the Playboy Club.

I was told there were approximately 115 males and 1200 females. They had plans to change it to an all-female FCI; the males would be shipped out at an undetermined date. I hoped not soon. There were women there from twenty to eighty years old. Most of the younger ones were in for small drug crimes; the older ones, mostly for embezzlement or fraud. There were a lot of Spanish-speaking girls from Columbia, Mexico, Bolivia and all over South America. Imelda Marcos from the Philippines was also housed there. She was the wife of Dictator Ferdinand Marcos who was also doing time in a high security prison in Illinois.

The dorms or housing units were clean and nice. They were built for the U.S. Public Health Department in 1935 for a drug hospital. The BOP took it over in 1972. It looked like a collage campus. No bars or cells. Air conditioned. We were free to roam about the compound. The men instructed to keep their hands off the girls. And they had the same instructions for the females. I guess you could have called this Club Med or Club Fed. We had movies every Saturday night; lots of recreation including a $1/3^{rd}$ mile track to run or walk on. There were three tennis courts, six racket ball courts and an indoor gym. "Membership" has its privileges. I guess the membership for this club was to commit a small federal crime.

It was quite a change from what I had been used to at the county jail. But I also felt bad about enjoying this fun in the sun with my loving wife and son at home trying to make ends meet. I did meet a couple of older men that seemed to be "professional prisoners." They loved it there. They had no family to worry about and in there they had no bills to pay, a nice place to eat and sleep with plenty of activities. I image they felt insecure on the outside.

I wanted to work in recreation. That was the slack job. Better than mowing grass or harder labor. I had been assigned to work as a unit orderly. I found out they wanted to start a soccer program and none of the employees knew anything about soccer. I had coached and refereed for ten years. So I was given the job of laying out the field and some of the inmates were assigned to help. All girls, of course; they had volunteered. Also, there was a lot of land, some of it was used for farming, raising the vegetables for the prison. Once a nice level area was selected for the field, we set up the soccer goals.

It took us almost five weeks before the field was ready. The team would be all female. Most were Latino and that was their national pastime. About twenty-five girls signed up. One of the gals who helped me the most was Bolivian. Her brother played pro for the Bolivian soccer team and she knew a lot about the game. Her English was also very good and she was a good interpreter. She was from a very well-to-do family in Bolivia that had large cattle ranch. These gals were all very good looking. And I was the only guy around them. They all wanted to put their hands on me but the Bolivian gal was kind of my body guard and she stayed close to me. She wanted to get something going between us; I must say it was tempting. Later another gal joined the team. She was from Fayetteville, N.C. She was a body builder and she had one that was custom built. She took a liking to me and, boy, that was tough. The Bolivian gal didn't like the extra female attention I was getting, but accepted it pretty well after I talked to her about being my assistant coach. The new gal said she was engaged to an Air Force pilot stationed at Fayetteville. But she was going to be here for three years. We sat and talked a lot about her family. They didn't have a lot of money when she was a child but managed to take a vacation once in a while. She had gotten involved with drugs in high school. She and some friends were caught with some coke and now they were doing time for possession.

In the cafeteria, we could talk and associate with the girls. It was not unusual for them to come and sit with us. Men were scarce and in demand.

There was one older lady from Kansas. She was a bank officer that was in for embezzling bank funds. Another female from Cincinnati, Ohio was working for a savings and loan and had been convicted on the same charge. Most of the Latin girls were in for smuggling drugs, mainly cocaine. They were called "Mules." Smugglers strap cocaine around their waist and send them to the U.S. by airline, usually multiple times. Some got through customs and some didn't. Some of the inmates just didn't have the willpower to keep their hands off the gals and they were receptive; but if caught in a sexual act, the men were shipped out to a higher level institution and the girls put in solitary for 30 days.

We got notice that all the men were going to be shipped out soon to make way for the all women's prison. The recreation director tried to get me to be one of the last to go but couldn't. About a week later the list came out. I was in the second shipment to go. All the soccer team girls gave me a party the night before and I was impressed. I don't know who took over the team after I left.

The next morning boarded the busses and left for Ft Worth, Texas. The trip to Ft Worth was long and tiresome. We called it the trip to "Wally World." It took almost seventeen hours. We were all restrained with handcuffs, leg irons and leg chains. Typical U.S. Marshal standard operating procedures. The bus was a steel cage inside. The steel doors inside were locked and there was no way anyone could get out. Even in an accident, we would all be doomed. No seat belts. There was really no reason for the cuffs and chains. We were all level one inmates.

Some of the men were sent on the airlift. It was a joke. They used an old (and I mean old) Boeing 727 that should have been scrapped long ago. It was a flying piece of junk. They secured them the same as we had been secured in the bus. Handcuffs and chains. The plane had more aborted takeoffs than a seagull in a hurricane. And there was not a direct flight. They stopped along the way, picking up and dropping off prisoners at each stop. While at the county jail in Kentucky a guy from St Louis I had gotten to know was shipped out to Lexington to catch the airlift. He wound up in El Reno, Oklahoma. His destination was Florida. There they gave him a bus ticket and told him to catch a bus to Tampa. Their travel agent must have failed geography.

We arrived at the FCI Ft Worth at night and we were all tired. They gave us room assignments. Mine was like the one I had in Lexington. This facility had been an old drug hospital too. It had been built at the same time for the U.S. Department of Health for drug rehabilitation. It had opened in 1935-1936. So, you see, the U.S. had a drug problem even then. This was a training center for the BOP food service. So I was looking forward to good food here.

The next morning I got up for breakfast and walked to the chow hall and, lo and behold, I saw that this was also a co-ed institution. Nice. However, after talking with some guys in the chow hall, I found out that the females would be shipped out to Lexington soon. Then this would become an all-male institution.

I was assigned a job in the purchasing dept. I typed up and saw all purchases made for this institution and how much money was spent and for what. It was such a waste of money. The new warden arrived in July; and he spent $20,000 in landscaping alone. I guess he didn't like his predecessor's yard. He also spent more dollars on remodeling the house. Inmates did a lot of the remodeling but the prison system paid for the material.

After I had been there a couple of weeks, they began bussing out the women. There were only about 150 females, not like Lexington. This would the all-male institution counterpart to Lexington's all-female institution. Lexington was a much larger place then this one. It could hold over 1800 inmates and Ft Worth about 750.

There I met some really interesting people: doctors, lawyers, CPA's, a few bank presidents and judges, to say the least. And a few Mexicans on small drug crimes that barely qualified as federal.

After a week there, an older guy and I had lunch. We talked a lot. He was from New Jersey. His name was Art. He was a member of the Gambino crime family. He was next to the consigliore (advisor) to the boss. Sometimes we ate lunch with a guy from another crime family. All these guys were really up in age. This guy was the consigliore to the Genovese crime family. Now these guys were not young. They were all in their late 70's or 80's. I used to walk on the track with Art. He didn't talk much about the old days. Still, we had some interesting conversations. There were a few more of the crime families there but the BOP was careful not to mix different families that were enemies. They were still enemies and could cause problems. Most were the soldiers and lower ranks and when they came in; when they were introduced to the consigliore, they would kneel and kiss his ring, still very loyal to the family. Reminded me of some scenes from *The Godfather*.

I heard some of the men were going back to Lexington to help with some of the heavy work that was required there. Of course everyone tried to get on the list but they only took twenty five. I wasn't one of them.

My appeal would be heard in oral arguments by the 6th Circuit Court of Appeals in Cincinnati, Ohio. One of my appeal issues was variance. This meant I was prejudiced by being tried with the other defendants. There were so many people being tried to testify against each other the jury couldn't sort out and recall who testified against whom, so they just found everyone guilty. This was in November and we hoped to get a decision by January.

I had been in the prison system for some time and had met more incompetent government employees than you can imagine. Most could not get a job on the outside. It seemed to me that they hired people who couldn't find employment elsewhere. There were a few exceptions, of course, but very few. Some were very nice but really slow in their thinking processes.

While in Lexington I had signed up to meet the parole board in October but was transferred in August to Ft Worth. My case manager in Ft Worth scheduled me for the October board there. My name was third from the top to appear on Monday. Monday came and by noon I hadn't been called. I saw her in the unit and she said they had misplaced my file but not to worry; they would find it by Friday. The parole board would be there all week. I saw her again on Thursday and found out the parole board had left Wednesday. She assured me she would set me up for the December board. What a disappointment.

I thought being born on the 11th of April was a lucky day but now I was thinking it wasn't so lucky. Now mind you these guidelines were set by the probation dept in Louisville at 24 to 36 months. I would be paroled in April 1988, making me eligible for a halfway house in October of 1988. So if the parole board had considered these guidelines I could leave any time. But now I was having to wait till December.

Later, I heard the parole board was coming back in November and I was all set to go. I had been assigned a new case manager (the other one was transferred); he gave me more bad news. The board sent a letter to the probation dept in Louisville asking for clarification on just what my involvement was in this conspiracy. They couldn't tell by reading my PSR (pre-sentence report). The report was prepared by the probation dept and attached in each prisoner's central file. So now I would have to wait till February 1989. It was in my sentencing order from the Judge and I pointed it out to him earlier when we reviewed my file. He looked surprised and highlighted the page. Now, I was set to see the board for next Tuesday. Tuesday came and went and I was informed the board didn't have time to read the file. This was just a small part of the crap we dealt with; the parole board didn't care. I would be scheduled later.

By that time, I hoped the court of appeals would rule in my favor either this month or next. I still had the other two indictments but they were double jeopardy and should have been ruled as such. The U.S. prefers not to rule like this as it could weaken their case on the others who have no jeopardy claim.

Christmas came and still no word. I called my attorney and he had already left for a two-week holiday. That night I called home and talked to my wife. She was crying a little. I knew she missed me but didn't understand why she was this sad. Maybe because we had not been together as a family for the holidays. I soon found out it was more than that. She thought the attorney had already informed me about the appeal. We had lost it. I was shocked. I had been so certain we would get the appeal. The next day I received the attorney's short letter in the mail and a copy of the court's opinion. Some Christmas gift. *"Bah-Humbug."*

I wrote a three-page letter to my attorney. I intended to appeal their decision because, in their opinion, they explained my involvement and it was nowhere near what was presented by the U.S. Attorney or my appeal brief. They weren't even close. So maybe, I thought, we could appeal their misconstrued opinion. I was quickly losing faith in the justice system.

By now I was really missing my wife and son. He was growing up and wanted to join the Marines. He had one year more of high school left. I wanted more time with him before he left home.

The holidays came and went and still no word from the court. And still, I had not seen the parole board. I needed to get the second charge out of the way and this was taking too long. My attorney said most of the other people plead out; if I could get a concurrent sentence starting the same date I might go ahead and do the same. Of course, this would depend on whether this attorney could cut a deal with the U.S. Attorney. He did. He said I could get a 5-6 year concurrent sentence starting when the first one began in May of 1987. So I told him to set it up. Soon, I would be on my way to Kentucky.

So in January of 1989 I was put on a bus and transported to El Reno, Oklahoma. El Reno was a high level security prison. I was put in a dorm-like building with other level one inmates. The different levels run from one to five. Five being the really bad guys. We could not leave this dorm. We could not mix with the other inmates that were higher level. This was also a prison for military prisoners. We were on the second floor and food was brought in by carts. Some of the smokers were calling down to inmates walking by below and bumming cigarettes. The smokers would drop a string down and they would tie cigarettes to them and then pull them up.

After eight days here a few of us were taken to the airport and put on the U.S. Marshal's airlift to go to Kentucky. The trip took the better part of the day, departing from El Reno at 5am, secured with chains and shackles. We landed at Lexington, Kentucky. Upon our arrival two U.S. Marshals were there to meet me and transport me to Louisville. I was held in the Jefferson county jail for four days before I had the opportunity to speak with the U.S. Attorney. We didn't talk much; he just asked a few questions. Three days later we met again and this time there was an IRS agent present. After two hours of questions he would only bargain for eight years. I was expecting five to six. There were five counts on the indictment and three were dismissed. *Eight years!* The attorney said the other charges would run concurrent and it wouldn't make any difference. My mistake, the parole board looks at it differently. They could extend your time in prison before parole or the halfway house was granted.

I left three days later on the Marshals airlift headed for El Reno. We had to go to Tampa, Florida to pick up some more prisoners. While we were still on the ground two prisoners slipped out of their handcuffs and chains and opened the escape hatch on the plane just over the wing. Usually one Marshal would stay on the plane and two or three outside until all prisoners were loaded. These guys slipped out on the wing and had planned to drop off after the other Marshals got onboard; then they planned to get away while the plane was taxiing out. Unfortunately for them, one of the pilots spotted them and they were put into the rear and watched closely.

Next stop was El Reno. I spent ten days here. This place was a federal holdover for inmates in transit. The next day they let us out in the exercise yard. I saw a guy, sitting in the sun, trying to keep warm. This was in February and it was a little chilly. He had no jacket, just a short sleeved shirt. He was a small frail-looking man about 65 years old. Had a small beard and was not dressed for cool weather. I had an army field jacket on and a long sleeved shirt. I took my jacket off and offered it to him and we struck up a conversation. I also noticed he had what looked like small sores or burn marks on his arms about the size of a cigarette. He introduced himself as Harry Rupp. He said he was from the Denver area. He had been in Leavenworth Prison for a while. Also he was a pilot and we talked for some time about flying. Then he told me he had been William Casey's pilot, employed by the CIA. William Casey had been director of the CIA back in the '70s. Before that, Harry had met Casey right after World War II ended. Casey was in military intelligence and hired him to go to work them then. He had been flying for Swiss Air. The CIA was formed and he continued on as Casey's pilot. Prior to becoming head of the CIA, Casey was rumored to have been a spy in the war and the cold war era after the war. He died in the '80s of cancer.

Rupp went on to say he flew Casey all over to different countries: Beirut, Iran, Paris, Switzerland and others. He said he was instrumental in setting up phony bank loans for the CIA and Casey. That is how the CIA got their slush fund money to finance uprisings such as the Nicaragua uprising with the Sandinista government. During this time, the Iran/Contra was making the news a lot. I know a little about the

Contra and Nicaragua situation. Harry had decided to skim a little for himself and that's what landed him in prison. They were doing this to banks and S&L's throughout the U.S. through phony companies with no intention of paying it back. He said he skimmed a little over three million dollars. He had been interrogated by the CIA just before I talked to him. He didn't say but I think the marks on his arms were burn marks. They wanted to know where the money was. He also said he was a German Luftwaffe pilot at 14 years old near the end of the war. Generally, the FBI tries to track down missing money, but the CIA was on this because it was their money that was missing.

I left the next day and would have liked to have talked to him more. I bet he knew a lot on Casey and one wonders what secrets Casey took to the grave with him.

I was put on the airlift the next day and sent back to Ft Worth. My wife and son came by a week later; they were moving to Phoenix, Arizona. She was driving a rental truck and towing an old VW bug behind it. That was the only car she had left. She already had a job there and a place to stay. Our daughter was married and lived in Phoenix. I really felt bad with me in this position and they were struggling to make ends meet. They wanted to get closer to me and this was closer than Louisville. Still, not close enough.

The next day I saw my case manager and asked if I could get closer to my wife in Phoenix. She said there was a camp in Boron, California that was closer. She would try to get me transferred there. But my wife had to have a residence established there before she could transfer me. It had to be approved by the BOP. I was hoping this case manager stayed here for a while. They changed constantly. I went back to work in the business office there and the employees seemed happy to see me back. We all got along well; this was a nice bunch of people that worked together well.

A few days later I was asked to go out and help unload a truck. It held about 30 boxes of office supplies. Three other inmates and I took about an hour to unload it. We never hurried and the driver and I struck up a conversation. He was from Minnesota and said his next stop was Iowa. He wanted to know if I would like to just stay in the truck behind some boxes up front of the trailer and go along. He said the guards at the gate only opened the back door, looked in, closed them and he would be off. "No thanks." But it sure was tempting! I hoped I wouldn't be in too much longer.

A couple of days later I heard from my wife and she settled down in an apartment in Arizona. She was working, or rather managing, a high end women's store in Scottsdale. She knows fashion for women well. I informed my case manager and she put in the paperwork for me to transfer to Boron, California. This was the closest BOP low level camp to the Phoenix area. About a week later she told me she was being transferred to upstate New York. *God, here we go again.* So now who was going to help me on my transfer to California?

CHAPTER EIGHTEEN

California

Two weeks later the unit manager called me into his office. He had received paperwork from the people at Boron wanting to know where I was. My transfer had been approved and without a case manager it was overlooked. Their communications were always a breakdown in the system. So, almost jumping with glee, I rushed to my room and started packing. The U.S. Marshals would be by to pick me up the next day. I quickly packed everything in a bag they provided which reminded me of the Air Force. Hurrying up and packing to ship out.

The U.S. Marshals picked me up the next morning about 6am and drove to the airport. We rode in their van for over two hours. These guys didn't get lost. I was boarded on the flying wreck and shackled up as before and we shook, rattled and rolled down the runway for takeoff. Then all of a sudden the power was cut, reverse thrust on the engines, heavy breaking and came to a stop. Turned around and taxied back. There was some kind of engine light blinking and we had to wait for a mechanic to fix the problem. After two hours, off we went again. We landed at El Reno; we didn't deplane this time, just picked up some more prisoners. We were on the ground about 30 minutes and off again. We stopped in San Diego, California to pick up more prisoners. Then off to Los Angeles where me and two others were taken off.

The U.S. Marshals met us, boarded us in a van and headed for Boron camp. One of the prisoners was from the LA area and we talked about the camp. He was in for bank fraud only and had two years to go. He said his family still lived in Los Angeles. The marshals were now looking at a map and didn't know just how to get to the camp from LA. The guy from LA said he knew the way and directed them on which highway to take. Our two-hour ride took over three hours, but finally we were there.

It was a camp with no fence, just a check-in guard shack at the entrance. We were checked in and were assigned barracks to live in. I had a room with an ex-army colonel. He didn't talk about why he was incarcerated. We got along well.

I went in the prison work industry called UNICORE. They had them at different intuitions and made different products. Here they made and rewound starters for cars and trucks. UNICORE is a big money maker for the prison system. They only paid the inmates, then, about .25 per hour. That made it easy for them to outbid retailers on contracts. Their cost was so low. I was in the supply department and later transferred to the warehouse. Here I was assigned more or less managerial duties. There was a BOP employee over me and the others but I pretty much ran the work schedule. I just told the BOP employee "Vince, here is the work schedule," and he would okay it. He wasn't there much. I had the keys to the warehouse. I picked up the van each morning at the motor pool and drove it to the warehouse. This was like a regular job; we just couldn't leave the compound. They had no filing system. It was totally a mess so I set up a file system. I opened all packages that were delivered to the camp. They were delivered to the main gate and I drove the van down and picked them up. One day I opened a long package with two automatic shotguns in it. This was a camp and you could walk off any time you wanted to; it was not like anyone would need them to shoot their way out. But I didn't think I should handle them. They were supposed to go the security department. I hid them in Vince's office and let him take them to security so they would think he opened them. He was really supposed to open all incoming packages. This guy was just lazy and didn't show up at the warehouse much. He thanked me for covering his butt and he took the guns down and delivered them to security.

We had a fire department crew and they covered the camp and surrounding area towns. Some inmates were trustees. As long as we were in for bed check each night all was well.

I was in the chow hall for lunch one day and saw a guy come in. He looked very familiar. When he sat down I went over at his table and it was Ed, the CIA pilot I flew with to Nicaragua. Ed had been at Leavenworth, Kansas for the past two years. They lowered his level and moved him to Boron. Ed said they didn't get to bring anything back that day because of the attack and they had to get out of there fast. What they were doing was taking guns down and bringing drugs back on some occasions. He said the CIA wanted something from a foreign government; they put out the word and if a drug smuggler obtained it and brought it back with a load of drugs it was fine. If they got caught it was hushed up and dismissed. The CIA knew who was smuggling drugs anyway. They never had to clear customs and had nothing to worry about. Ed thought it looked so easy he decided to skim a little for himself but got caught trying to sell it. He had two more years to do before he would be released. I told him I should be leaving soon and suggested he try to get in the warehouse as it was an easy job. I only saw him off and on for the next few weeks before I was released.

My wife and son came frequently to visit. It was great getting to see them regularly. They were doing okay. My son was in a trade school in Phoenix. My daughter and her husband came out also. This was much better than before. I had missed my family a lot.

One guy had a visit with his wife and decided to leave with her. They went into town and were found in a local motel. The police picked him up and brought him back. He was gone over 24 hours and considered an escapee; 5 years were added to his sentence. He was shipped out to a higher level institution, one with a fence around it and higher security. The sad thing about this was he only had six months left before he would have been released. Some just cannot resist the temptation. I also had a friend in Chino, California who came to visit from time to time. He and I had shared an apartment in St Louis when we were both single. He then worked for Broyhill Furniture Company. They shipped him out to California and he has been there since.

Some of the other inmates included five judges that were caught in a bribery sting in California. I played tennis with a couple of them. Yes, we had three tennis courts and two racket ball courts. They advised me on some of my legal avenues to get my sentence reduced. Good advice which I passed along to my attorney. He talked to one of the judges by phone one day and finally my sentence was reduced from eight years to 62 months. I had been in just under five years. Time was passing. I was probably in the best health I'd been in a long time. I ate good and walked the track a lot. I did a lot of thinking of what I was going to do when I was released. The court still had my pilot's license. I didn't know if I would or could go back to flying, maybe as a hobby, but not as a business again. I had been out of the business for awhile, I would have a lot of catching up to do if any FAA regulations had changed.

I wrote the FAA in Oklahoma City for a copy of my license and their answer was my license had been revoked, not suspended as I had hoped. This meant I would have to take all my test and certifications over again. I learned that once you are convicted of a felony the FAA revokes your license.

As I waited for my release, I remembered flying to so many interesting places and how much I had enjoyed being a pilot. I probably will never have the chance to fly to such exotic places again. I remember my first trip to Belize to pick up an airplane for an individual from Paducah, Kentucky. It was my first long trip out of the U.S. I just liked the challenge and the adventure. A guy had been down on vacation with family and the fuel pump went out on his plane. They all flew home on a commercial flight. After about 4 weeks the plane was ready to be picked up; he called me. He couldn't take time off work. I jumped at the chance to take the trip. I arrived commercial by a Guatemalan airline. This plane was in about the same shape as the U.S. Marshals plane. They served hot salsa dip and chips on the flight.

The airplane I was picking up was a single engine Cessna 210. I had a lot of time in this type of plane and wasn't worried about flying it. I paid for the repairs and checked the plane over really well. Then I flew the plane down the coast for about ten miles staying near the beach so if the engine quit I could land it there. Everything seemed to check out and I planned to leave the next morning and go north to Merida, Mexico, land for fuel then head north to New Orleans, Louisiana.

Taking off the next morning I noticed the airspeed indicator wasn't working. It worked fine the day before but I just wanted to leave this place. I didn't feel comfortable here so I let it go for now. I landed at Merida, Mexico and found the problem. An insect had built a dirt nest in the pitot-static tube. The pitot-static tube is a tube that sticks out of the wing with a small hole in it to measure the air pressure; it gives a reading on the airspeed indicator. I fixed it and left for the trip across the Gulf to New Orleans. I cleared customs and they checked the plane over good because this type of plane is frequently used by smugglers. I was cleared and the trip was uneventful all the way to Louisville.

I had my memories and time seemed to pass by quickly as long as I stayed busy. Finally, my day to be released arrived and I was processed. My wife picked me up to take me to a halfway house in Phoenix. It was February 1992 now. I checked in and was told I would spend two weeks here before being released with no probation. I would be a free man. I smiled.

My friend in Chino, California said he would hire me if I could move to California near him. It sounded good. My wife applied for a store manager for a large baby clothing store chain and got the job. After leaving the halfway house, I moved with my wife to Rancho Cucamonga, California. Now we could finally resume our life together.

Am I glad I did what I did? No, I am not proud of it. The thrill and excitement was the way it started out. And I kept getting in deeper and deeper. I knew how to get in the U.S. without detection, by flying under the radar. I didn't intend for it to develop into what it did. I didn't get convicted on what I did, just selling an airplane to Garner who died of cancer about two years after the trial was over.

I learned that no matter how much you change your life you have to pay a price for what you've done. I paid mine. I put my wife and son through some very hard times. However, she proved to be a champion; she made it work. Through it all, she stuck by me and was there when I got out. Although, I didn't get caught for some of the things I did, there was no real evidence against me, so maybe the time I served was God's way of punishing me for what I did do. I am really proud of my wife and thankful that now we can enjoy a normal life together. How sweet it is.

Flying Under the Radar

Al Isley

ABOUT THE AUTHOR

Born and raised in North Carolina, Al Isley is the son of a hard working farmer and a school teaching mother. Today, he lives in Myrtle Beach, S.C. with his wife. In his spare time he enjoys working in the tourist industry. He has his pilot's license and does some private flying… just for fun.

Made in the USA
Lexington, KY
28 January 2015